JAMESTOWN EDUCATION

Teaching Reading with Jamestown

Strategies and Instruction

Mc Graw Hill **Glencoe**

New York, New York   Columbus, Ohio   Chicago, Illinois   Peoria, Illinois   Woodland Hills, California

JAMESTOWN EDUCATION

Acknowledgments

Aaron, Ira E. "Enriching the Basal Reading Program with Literature." *Children's Literature in the Reading Program.* Ed. Bernice E. Cullinan. Newark, DE: International Reading Association, 1987. 126–138.

Duffy, Gerald G., Laura R. Roehler, and Beth Ann Herrmann. "Modeling Mental Processes Helps Poor Readers Become Strategic Readers." *The Reading Teacher,* 1988 (April): 762–767

Farnan, Nancy, and Alicia Romero. "Understanding Literature." *Content Area Reading and Learning* (2nd ed.). Ed. Diane Lapp, James Flood, and Nancy Farnan. Needham Heights, MA: Allyn & Bacon, 1996. 209–225.

Fielding, Linda G., and P. David Pearson. "Reading Comprehension: What Works." *Educational Leadership,* 1994 (February).

Laflamme, J. G. "The Effect of the Multiple Exposure Vocabulary Method and the Target Reading/Writing Strategy on Test Scores." *Journal of Adolescent and Adult Literacy* 40 (1997): 372–381.

L'Engle, Madeleine. *Herself: Reflections on a Writing Life.* Colorado Springs: Shaw Books, 2001.

Monson, Dianne. "Characterization in Literature: Realistic and Historical Fiction." *Children's Literature in the Reading Program.* Ed. Bernice E. Cullinan. Newark, DE: International Reading Association, 1987. 98–110.

Palincsar, Annemarie Sullivan, and Ann L. Brown. "Reciprocal Teaching of Comprehension-Fostering and Comprehension-Monitoring Activities." *Cognition and Instruction* 1:2 (1984): 117–175.

Paris, Scott G., Marjorie Y. Lipson, and Karen K. Wixson. "Becoming a Strategic Reader." *Contemporary Educational Psychology* 8 (1983). In *Theoretical Models and Processes of Reading.* Ed. Robert B. Ruddell, Martha Rapp Ruddell, Harry Singer. Newark, DE: International Reading Association, 1994. 788–810.

Rhoder, Carol. "Mindful Reading: Strategy Training That Facilitates Transfer." *Journal of Adolescent and Adult Literacy* 45:6 (2002): 498–513.

Tovani, Cris. *I Read It, but I Don't Get It: Comprehension Strategies for Adolescent Readers.* Portland, ME: Stenhouse Publishers, 2000.

 **Glencoe**

The **McGraw-Hill** Companies

Send all inquiries to:

Glencoe/McGraw-Hill
8787 Orion Place
Columbus, OH 43240-4027

ISBN: 0-07-845747-5

1 2 3 4 5 6 7 8 9 10 113 09 08 07 06 05 04 03

Table of Contents

Reading with Jamestown

Jamestown Placement Test

IRA/NCTE Standards for the English Language Arts

Glossary

Graphic Organizers

Teaching Reading

Teaching Reading with Jamestown provides the teaching support you need for the teaching of reading. Whether you are a professional in the field of reading or an instructor whose specialization lies elsewhere, using this guide will help you to maximize your students' abilities and to augment their reading skills.

What's provided in this guide?

▶ teaching techniques—such as reciprocal teaching and modeling—for presenting reading instruction

▶ a schedule of all the necessary "ingredients" for a successful reading program

▶ strategies designated for each phase of the reading lesson cycle—before reading, during reading, and after reading

▶ step-by-step minilessons for teaching key reading skills and strategies

▶ modeled use of graphic organizers

▶ student handouts of strategy reminders and strategy applications

with Jamestown

Consult this guide to do the following:

- ✔ construct effective three-part reading lessons
- ✔ find strategies that will improve your students' fluency and comprehension
- ✔ find techniques to develop your students' vocabulary
- ✔ develop varied cooperative learning situations for students
- ✔ determine students' placement in Jamestown materials
- ✔ check classroom goals against the reading standards proposed by IRA/NCTE
- ✔ make optimal use of Jamestown reading products

Key Components of Reading Instruction

Reading is a learned process, and increasing proficiency in reading requires focused instruction and practice in key areas. An effective reading program incorporates into a weekly schedule the following five elements.

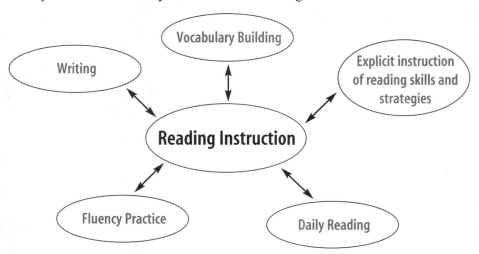

Vocabulary Building

Recognizing words and knowing their meanings help ensure comprehension and speed reading. To prepare students to read a selection, engage them in a vocabulary building activity that will help them master key words they will encounter in the selection. Many Jamestown reading programs, such as the Signature Reading series, supply a list of key vocabulary words with each reading selection. If you are selecting your own vocabulary words from a reading selection, choose four to seven words that are critical to your students' understanding of the selection.

Memory Techniques

When students are presented with new vocabulary words, have them use the words in ways that will make the words and their definitions memorable. Students may use any of the following techniques to help them remember a vocabulary word and its definition.

- **Draw it.** Students sketch what a vocabulary word represents. For example, if the vocabulary word were *osprey,* students would sketch a hawk.

"In the last 10 years, researchers have acclaimed vocabulary knowledge as the single most important factor in reading comprehension."
—J. G. Laflamme,
"The Effect of the Multiple Exposure Vocabulary Method and the Target Reading/Writing Strategy on Test Scores." *Journal of Adolescent and Adult Literacy*

- **Write it.** Students write the word and explore its meaning in writing. They might answer these questions about the word: What does it mean? What is it like? What are some examples?
- **Manipulate it.** Students interact with the word in as many ways as possible. They might use the word in any of the following ways:

List rhyming words.	Create a web of associated words.
List opposites.	Break the word into word parts.
List synonyms.	Write a sentence using the word.

Vocabulary Activities

Three vocabulary minilessons—Fix-Up Word Strategies, Context Clues, and Word Parts—(pp. 28–35) will help you provide your students with instruction and practice in using important vocabulary skills and strategies. In addition, the following activities can help students explore words and remember them.

Word Tables Students can create three-column tables and record words, definitions, and hand-drawn illustrations that will help them remember the meanings of words.

Vocabulary Word	Information	Memory Clue
vitality	enthusiasm and energy to "get up and go"	Go!
tsunami	a flooding wave caused by an earthquake at sea	Earthquake
exultation	expressing great happiness or joy	Yippiee! Hooray! Fantastic! Way to go!

> **Teaching Tip**
>
> Have students complete vocabulary activities and record new words and their definitions in a vocabulary notebook— a simple spiral notebook designated for vocabulary use.

Word Grids Students can use a Word Grid to make connections and build associations with words. In each box of the grid, students use the vocabulary word in a different way. Students might begin by defining the word and then create a drawing of what the word represents. They might use the word in a sentence, break the word into syllables, create a rhyme or rap for the word, and think of as many antonyms, synonyms, and word associations for the word as they can.

Antonym joy	Rhyme *Much to the lawyer's* *<u>consternation</u>,* *He had overlooked* *important legislation.*	Illustration Uh-oh!
Meaning *dismay or* *concern, often* *caused by some-* *thing unexpected* *or confusing*	**consternation**	Example *Not being able to* *find one's term* *paper can cause* *<u>consternation</u>.*
Synonyms *alarm* *fright*	In Syllables *con ster na tion*	Used in a Sentence *The upcoming* *final exam caused* *great <u>consterna-</u>* *<u>tion</u> among the* *students.*

Word Box Being empowered to select their own vocabulary words helps motivate students to learn new words. When students come across unfamiliar words as they read a selection, have them contribute the words to a class Word Box. To contribute to the Word Box, students fill out a slip of paper with the following information: the word, its definition, the selection title, and the number of the page on which the word was found. Students sign their contributions. After all students have finished reading the selection, draw words from the box and ask the class (except for the contributor) to guess the meaning of each word. If necessary, have the contributor of the word slip supply the word's definition for the class.

Teaching Tip

Reinforce students' choices of words for the Word Box by using the vocabulary words they have selected in additional vocabulary activities.

Tony Rodriguez
murky: thick with dirt or smoke and difficult to see through
—*The Wild Side: Total Panic*, "A Deadly Plunge," page 39

Explicit Instruction of Reading Skills and Strategies

Comprehension is a cognitive process, and therefore "invisible." Unlike someone who repairs a bicycle, a reader cannot study his or her own reading
process and observe what part, if any, is "broken" and is causing a lack of
understanding of what has been read. Less-proficient readers are often
unaware of *when* their understanding breaks down, *why* it breaks down, and
how to repair it. Therefore, explicit instruction of reading skills and strategies
is essential. Explicit instruction is instruction that explains, step by step, how
to solve a specific reading problem. The teacher selects an appropriate reading
strategy and explains why the strategy was chosen and how to use it. The
teacher then models using the strategy by thinking aloud and actively working
through the reading problem. The goal of explicit instruction is to provide students with complete instruction—through explanation, modeling, and thinking
aloud—that directly addresses a reading problem. Ultimately the process is
turned over to the students, and they use what they have learned as they practice using the strategy when they encounter similar reading problems.

Explicit instruction will take up one-quarter to one-third of the scheduled
time in a reading class. Many Jamestown programs, such as Signature
Reading, incorporate into the student lessons explicit instruction in reading
strategies. Teaching or reviewing the appropriate skill or strategy lessons with
students before they read a selection can enhance their understanding of the
text. Explicit instruction for several core reading strategies is provided in
Teaching Reading with Jamestown on pages 26–65.

> "We know that good readers use more strate-gies as they read and they use them more effectively than poor readers."
> –Scott G. Paris, Marjorie Y. Lipson, and Karen K. Wixson, "Becoming a Strategic Reader." *Contemporary Educational Psychology*

Daily Reading

Because reading is a skill acquired through practice, a liberal amount of class
time should be allotted for students to participate in the actual process of reading. Students might read orally or silently, independently or with a group.
Jamestown's high-interest reading series, such as Critical Reading Series and
The Wild Side, will help engage all readers (but especially reluctant readers) in
daily reading practice. A reasonable guideline for the scheduling of reading time
is twenty minutes per day, or one-quarter to one-third of the weekly class time.

Fluency Practice

To read with ease and expression, readers need to work on a passage the way
that musicians work on a song—by *practicing* it.

What Is Fluency? Fluency is smooth, accurate reading at a steady pace.
Fluent readers see words in large, meaningful groupings. Their reading sounds
like conversation—smooth, quick, and expressive. Choppy reading is the
opposite of fluent reading; it is a stop-and-start process in which words are
read in isolation, one at a time.

> "The major aim of read-ing instruction programs is to develop readers who not only *can* read but who *do* read and who will continue to read through-out life."
> –Ira E. Aaron, "Enriching the Basal Reading Program with Literature." In *Children's Literature in the Reading Program*

Purpose of Fluency Practice Fluency practice helps students in these ways:
- by focusing attention on the sound of language when spoken smoothly
- by providing concrete steps that lead to improvement in reading aloud
- by increasing students' confidence in their reading abilities as they move away from a slow, painstaking approach and "get into the flow" of language
- by improving students' comprehension as they read whole phrases, or "chunks of meaning," instead of isolated words

Repeating Readings In the classroom, fluency is achieved primarily through *repeated oral readings.* Just as musicians cannot be expected to play a piece perfectly after only playing it through once, readers must practice reading a passage to gain proficiency. During the first "run-through" of a selection, developmental readers often struggle to decode words and to discover meaningful phrasing. Each repeated practice session, however, helps them move beyond the fundamentals.

Fluency practice can easily be incorporated into a reading program schedule. At least twice weekly fluency practice is recommended. Jamestown's Reading Fluency series provides students with all of the materials they need to practice gaining fluency on a weekly schedule. Another Jamestown product well suited to fluency practice is the Timed Readings series, which provides short interesting selections, at specific reading levels, in a format geared to timing. Use the following procedure to have your students practice to attain increased fluency.

Twice-Weekly Fluency Practice

The teacher . . .
1. pairs students
2. provides students with copies of a high-interest passage that is about 200 words in length
3. times students as one person, and then the other, of each pair reads aloud for one minute; then repeats the timing process for a second round of reading

Students . . .
1. each read the passage aloud to a partner; partners take turns reading aloud
2. mark how far they got in the passage when time was called by initialing the point at which they stopped, followed by the number 1 or 2 to indicate which reading attempt they are making
3. answer these questions to evaluate their own fluency after completing each reading:
   a. On a scale from 1 to 5, with 5 being smooth and 1 being choppy, how smoothly did I read?
   b. On a scale from 1 to 5, with 5 being expressive and 1 being not expressive, how expressively did I read?
   c. What, if anything, presented a problem during reading? Why?

Writing

Because the skills of reading and writing both make use of the written word, increasing skill in one area often increases ability in the other area. Hence, written literacy reinforces reading literacy and vice versa. In addition, writing is an excellent "thinking tool," helping students to organize, synthesize, and develop their ideas.

"Quickwrites"—freewriting on a topic for one to five minutes—can be smoothly incorporated into any part of a reading class. One effective use of quickwrites is to have students jot down ideas on a topic or question they will encounter in their reading. After they have read, students can use their quickwrites, as well as their newly acquired story knowledge, as an aid in discussing the selection.

Another important form of student writing is the personal response, in which students react in writing to what they have read. Students are more readily engaged in reading when they feel that their reactions to the text are important.

Varied writing opportunities—ranging from informal to formal, from jotted notes to polished essays—allow students to explore a reading selection. During, or especially after, they read, students might write any of the following, using in some way the information from the selection.

> "Research of the past fifteen years in reading and writing suggests that instructional integration of reading and writing can increase students' reading, writing, and thinking skills."
> —Nancy Farnan and Alicia Romero, "Understanding Literature." In *Content Area Reading and Learning*

Writing Activities

character sketch	book review
news story	interview
journal entry	summary
captions	job description
outline	sequel
poem	description
script	ad
comic strip	dialogue
editorial	brochure
personal response	notes

Writing is reinforced in many Jamestown reading programs, especially the Best series and Five-Star Stories. The Fright Write series presents high-interest, long-term writing projects. In Fright Write, students follow a step-by-step process, completing smaller writing assignments as they progress toward creating such products as a scary story, a comic book, an audiotape, or a play script.

Classroom Management

Arranging a weekly schedule of instruction, choosing effective teaching methods, selecting appropriate student groupings, and planning student conferences are all part of classroom management.

Organizing Instruction

Your weekly plan for teaching reading should incorporate the five key components of instruction (vocabulary building, explicit instruction in reading strategies, daily reading, fluency practice, and writing). Instruction or practice in using strategies is presented in many Jamestown reading series, including Signature Reading and the Best series. Following is a standard organizational plan for teaching reading.

Sample Organizational Plan

Day	Instructional Activity	Time Allotment	Description
One	Explicit instruction; use of graphic organizer	20 minutes	Present reading strategy instruction, including modeled use of the strategy. For strategy minilessons, see pages 26–65 in this guide or use the strategy instruction provided in a Jamestown reading program. When appropriate, introduce a graphic organizer that reinforces the skill or strategy instruction.
	Guided reading; use of graphic organizer or writing activity	30 minutes	Guide students to apply the strategy to a brief reading selection. Discuss the strategy application. Then have students complete the graphic organizer or a writing activity related to the reading.
Two	Before- and during-reading activities; vocabulary activity; guided reading	full session	Begin a complete reading lesson, using before- and during-reading strategies and activities from this guide or from a Jamestown series. Include a vocabulary activity. During guided reading, call on students to apply the strategy or skill they learned on Day One.

Day	Instructional Activity	Time Allotment	Description
Three	After-reading activities; follow-up activities; vocabulary activity; writing activity	full session	Complete the reading lesson begun on Day Two. Engage students in reviewing, responding to, and discussing the selection. Have students complete after-reading exercises. They may follow up on earlier activities—for example, by verifying their predictions or completing graphic organizers. Review selection vocabulary. Incorporate a writing activity.
Four	Daily reading; strategy practice; writing activity	30 minutes	Provide a brief reading selection well suited to the strategy taught on Day One and have students, independently or with partners, practice applying the strategy. Incorporate a writing activity.
	Fluency practice	20 minutes	Use Jamestown's Reading Fluency series or have students follow the fluency practice procedure outlined on page 6.
Five	Fluency practice; assessment	20 minutes	Use Jamestown's Reading Fluency series or have students follow the fluency practice procedure outlined on page 6.
	Outside reading; conferences	30 minutes	Have students read books of their choice as you meet individually with them about reading problems and goals.

Instructional Methods

Students are more likely to improve in reading when they are involved participants in the process. Both reciprocal teaching and modeling are instructional methods that call upon students to take increasing ownership of the reading process.

Reciprocal Teaching

Reciprocal teaching is an instructional method characterized by
- a reciprocal dialogue between teacher and students, and ultimately among students in a group, in which students take turns in the role of dialogue leader
- the construction of meaning by using four reading strategies: *summarizing, questioning, clarifying,* and *predicting.*

Four Strategies of Reciprocal Teaching

Summarizing   Readers identify the most important information in a segment of text and state that information in their own words. Summarizing involves students in recognizing and communicating the significant ideas in a text.

Questioning   Readers ask themselves questions about the text segment. Self-questioning aids comprehension by helping students identify where their understanding of the text has broken down and what they still need to know in order to understand what they have read.

Clarifying   Readers try to find answers to the questions they have raised and to make sense of parts of the text that have caused confusion. They seek clarification by rereading, reading ahead, or by seeking outside help, such as through a peer or a reference source.

Predicting   Readers tell what they think will happen next, basing their predictions on evidence from the text that they have already read.

"Charles' ability to generate questions continued to improve on each day of reciprocal teaching, as did his summarization skills."
—Annemarie Sullivan Palincsar and Ann L. Brown, "Reciprocal Teaching of Comprehension-Fostering and Comprehension-Monitoring Activities." *Cognition and Instruction*

Teaching students the reciprocal-teaching process involves a sequence of scaffolded instruction that moves students from teacher-dependence to self-monitored independence. After students learn the process of reciprocal teaching in a teacher-directed whole-class activity, they can effectively make use of the process in small groups, with a student dialogue leader in charge of guiding the group to apply the strategies. The four teaching steps, or scaffolds, of this technique follow.

Scaffolds of Reciprocal Teaching

First scaffold	**Explicit instruction**	The teacher defines each of the four reading strategies and explains how each is used.
Second scaffold	**Modeling**	The teacher selects a reading passage of one-half to one page in length and models how to use the four strategies by "thinking aloud."
Third scaffold	**Teacher-led discussion**	Students read the next text passage of one-half to one page in length. Teacher assists students in using the four strategies by asking pertinent questions and supplying answers or ideas when necessary.
Fourth scaffold	**Independent student use**	In small groups, students read a passage aloud and take turns summarizing, questioning, clarifying, and predicting while they discuss the text.

Modeling

An important element of strategic instruction is teacher modeling. As a part of the modeling process, teachers think aloud as they apply a reading strategy to solve a reading problem. In this technique, teachers give voice to the inner conversation that readers have with the text and demonstrate the strategy they used to understand their reading. To construct a "think-aloud," the teacher reads aloud a certain passage, stopping at pertinent points to talk about what he or she is thinking. A think-aloud demonstrates the cognitive process and allows students to observe how a proficient reader approaches a problem with reading. Three guidelines govern modeling and creating think-alouds: Keep thinking aloud *simple, logical,* and *step by step.* Several examples of think-alouds are included in the minilessons on pages 26–65.

"To model cognitive activity, teachers must make their reasoning visible to the novice."
–Gerald G. Duffy, Laura R. Roehler, and Beth Ann Herrmann, "Modeling Mental Processes Helps Poor Readers Become Strategic Readers." *The Reading Teacher*

Instructional Groupings

Students can read and discuss literature in several learning arrangements. Each method of grouping has its own unique benefits. Students can participate in independent, paired, small-group, or whole-class activities.

Cooperative Learning Methods

"In cooperative learning groups, each student contributes to the entire group's exploration and comprehension of text."
–Beverly Ann Chin, Professor of English, University of Montana

Young adult learners often benefit from working with their peers—either in pairs or in small groups. Following are recommended cooperative learning activities that may be used in a reading classroom.

Think-Pair-Share This collaborative method adds depth to class discussion by giving students an opportunity to explore and then to share their thoughts and ideas. In addition, students benefit from verbalizing their thoughts in a group and receiving the group's feedback. The method works in these three steps.

1. *Think:* The teacher presents a critical thinking problem—one that requires reflection, analysis, evaluation, or synthesis. (Jamestown reading programs suggest critical thinking questions after most reading selections.) Students take a minute to *think* about their personal response to the problem. (Quickwrites might be used here as a concrete thinking-by-writing tool.)
2. *Pair:* Students work with a partner, discussing and refining their responses.
3. *Share:* The class regroups for a follow-up discussion, and individuals share their responses with the group.

Interview Pairs To use this technique, learners collaborate as they complete the following steps.

1. *First-Partner Interview:* Pairs are formed or assigned. One student in each pair *interviews* the other by asking questions about a topic of discussion. The interview helps the partner explore and express ideas.
2. *Second-Partner Interview:* Partners switch roles. The interviewer becomes the interviewee.
3. *Pair-plus-Pair Interaction:* Each pair joins one other pair. The four members in the new group share their ideas.

Jigsaw A jigsaw collaboration is best employed for multifaceted learning or research projects, such as the extension exercises that often follow selections in Jamestown reading programs.

1. Divide the class into three or four "learning teams." Each team member is responsible for learning about and becoming an "expert" on one part of a reading assignment or a research project.

2. Distribute "expert" sheets to the learning teams. Each expert sheet identifies a focus or topic. For example, an expert sheet might require answers to questions on character development in a story; another expert sheet might require listing details that indicate the time period of the story.

3. Across the teams, those who were given the same expert sheet meet. They gather the required information—from their textbooks or from other specified sources. Then students return to their learning teams and teach team members what they have learned.

4. Students complete a written quiz to verify their understanding of all the information presented.

Conferencing

Developmental readers benefit from receiving feedback from the teacher that is explicit, substantial, and positive. Impromptu teacher-student conferences can be held with individuals or small groups while the remaining students are engaged in other meaningful work, such as in silent reading or completing written exercises. Frequent teacher-student conferences are recommended to accomplish the following goals.

Purposes of Conferencing

- To help students set specific long- and short-range learning goals.
- To help students assess their problem areas and determine specific solutions.
- To help students assess their learning strengths and to highlight how these assets can best be utilized.
- To monitor student progress.
- To discuss scores, including those from assessment checks, timed-reading graphs, and course exercises.
- To provide positive feedback and encouragement.

Anecdotal notes taken during observations of student reading can be helpful for providing specific feedback to students during conferences. Additionally, the teacher may check for fluency by asking the student to read aloud. Pointing out the student's strengths after reading provides encouragement, and focusing on one or two key tasks that will improve the student's reading provides the student with specific goals.

The teacher should invite the student to set one or more reading goals, and then designate and record the reading goals for the student. These might include consistently applying a specific decoding principle, mastering new vocabulary words, completing a graphic organizer, or practicing to achieve fluency of a segment of text. Students should receive a written copy of the reading goals that were developed during the reading conference.

Lesson Planning

Effective reading strategies and activities help students understand what they read. To create meaningful lessons, it is important to plan which strategies to use. Many strategies and activities are especially appropriate for use at specific stages of the reading lesson—before reading, during reading, or after reading. Some reading activities, such as completing a KWL chart, require the use of strategies over the course of the entire reading lesson.

Before Reading

Have students utilize the following four strategies before they read a selection:

Acquire critical vocabulary   Preview the selection
Activate prior knowledge   Set a purpose for reading

To guide students through the process of using these strategies, review the information that follows.

Acquire Critical Vocabulary

Preteaching key words that students will encounter in the reading selection will increase their understanding of what they read. The term "critical vocabulary" refers to the words that students must know in order to understand a selection. For example, before reading an article about toxic waste, students should be introduced to the critically important word *toxic*. Besides aiding comprehension, a preview of critical vocabulary helps focus students' attention and interest on the topic. (Vocabulary activities on pages 2–4 and vocabulary skills and strategies minilessons on pages 28–35 will help you teach students the selection vocabulary.)

Activate Prior Knowledge

The purpose of activating prior knowledge is to have students discover what they already know about the topic of a selection and its key ideas. As students share ideas, their interest is piqued. This helps focus their attention and in turn prepares them for acquiring new information as they read.

To activate students' prior knowledge, brainstorm with them. Ask students leading questions that are specific to the text they will read. For example, for a selection about the giant squid, ask students what they know about the giant squid. Have they ever seen one? In what setting? How did it look? How did it act? Was its appearance frightening? Or, if no one has seen one, ask such questions as "What do you think it would look like?" and "Have you ever read about such a creature or seen it in a movie?"

As students offer ideas, record them in a concept web on the board. Recording ideas gives weight to students' contributions.

Following is an example of a concept web recording students' prior knowledge about the giant squid.

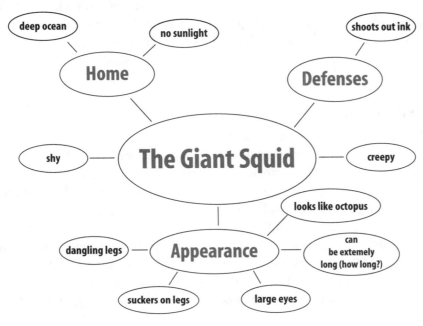

Preview the Selection

Previewing is the process of paging through a selection before reading in order to get an idea of what the text is about. Students should quickly preview the text elements listed below. Noting these elements will help them approach the text with the right cognitive tools.

General Text Elements	Additional Text Elements for Nonfiction
Title and subtitle Author's name First paragraphs Illustrations, captions Footnotes Words that stand out on the page	Headings and subheadings Graphics (photographs, charts, graphs, tables, maps) Sidebars, boxed notes Boldface terms

Set a Purpose for Reading

Setting a purpose for reading provides each student with a personal goal for reading a selection. Students set purposes for reading when they ask themselves what they hope to find out from their reading—they may want to learn more about a topic, find the answer to a question, or "get to know" a character. They may wonder how a situation mentioned while the class was engaged in activating prior knowledge relates to what they will read.

During Reading

To support your students' comprehension, suggest the use of appropriate strategies while students are engaged in reading. Then explain and model the application of those strategies. Also, choose the most appropriate way for your students to read each selection. By varying the way selections are read, you help heighten your students' interest and increase their motivation to read well.

Guided Reading

Guided reading is teacher-supported reading. It can take place in whole-class or small-group settings, or on a one-to-one basis between student and teacher. The role of the teacher is to provide guidance to the reader—by asking questions and pointing out clues in the text that will help the student answer questions and grasp key ideas. During guided reading, the teacher may find appropriate moments to teach the student (and the group) how and when to apply a reading strategy that will help make the text more manageable. As the student applies the strategy, the teacher is on hand to offer instant and specific feedback to the student's efforts. At the teacher's discretion, other members of the reading group may be allowed to also offer guidance and support to the reader.

During reading sessions, the teacher can provide a model of fluent and expressive reading by taking a turn within the group and participating in oral reading.

The teacher has the opportunity during student reading to assess the student's strengths and weaknesses and the progress the student has made toward specific reading goals. The teacher may plan one-to-one reading sessions with some or all students. Such sessions provide opportunities for individualized instruction in reading skills and strategies, and for evaluation and assessment of the student.

Reading Arrangements

You may choose to have students read in any of the following ways:

- *Guided reading:* students take turns reading aloud; teacher-directed
- *Silent individual reading:* students read silently
- *Paired reading:* partners read to each other
- *Choral reading:* groups are assigned to read, in unison, segments of text, according to an arrangement by a group leader
- *Echo reading:* a leader models reading a line or passage; the group repeats, or echoes, the reading of the same text
- *Radio reading:* after practicing, students each read aloud a segment of text as group members listen with books closed; then the reader asks the group a question about the section just read

> "I started to 'fake-read' in sixth grade. . . . [I] could decode even the most difficult words. The problem surfaced when I had to use, remember, or retell what I had read. I couldn't do it."
>
> —Cris Tovani,
> *I Read It but I Don't Get It:*
> *Comprehension Strategies for*
> *Adolescent Readers*

Lesson Planning

Six Active Reading Strategies

Active reading strategies are strategies that efficient readers automatically use during the process of reading. Encourage students to use the following six active reading strategies as they read text. During guided reading, stop at strategic points to model the use of the strategies.

- Monitor comprehension
- Solve reading problems
- Connect
- Comment
- Picture
- Predict

Active Reading Strategies	Teacher Resources for Instruction	Examples of Strategy Use
Monitor comprehension	Teach minilesson "Monitoring Comprehension," pages 26–27.	Hmm, this part is confusing. Ricky was rowing out to the deep water alone. All of a sudden he was with his brother on the lake.
Solve reading problems	Teach minilesson "Monitoring Comprehension," pages 26–27.	Oh, I get it. When I reread, I realize that Ricky is remembering a scary fishing trip with his brother. This must be a flashback.
Connect	See "Making Connections," page 20.	If I were Ricky, I'd be scared, because I know it's not safe to be out in the open during a severe thunderstorm.
Comment	Teach minilesson "Monitoring Comprehension," pages 26–27. See Responding, page 19.	I think the character is acting foolishly. He wants to prove himself, but for what?
Picture	Teach minilesson "Visualizing," pages 64–65.	I'm picturing this scene in my mind, and it looks scary—black skies, jagged lightning bolts, gray choppy waves.
Predict	Teach minilesson "Predicting," pages 36–38.	Ricky is ignoring the danger signs. I wonder whether he'll get into trouble.

Name _____

Cut out and fold the bookmark. Refer to the information on the bookmark to help you remember important reading strategies.

cut and fold

JAMESTOWN EDUCATION

Six Strategies to Use During Reading

▪ Monitor Comprehension
Do I get it?
Did my understanding break down?
If so, where?

▪ Solve Reading Problems
How do I fix the problem?
Do I reread, read ahead, or ask for help?

▪ Connect
How does this text relate to what I know?
How does my life connect to the text?
Have I ever had a similar experience
 or feeling?

▪ Comment
What notes do I want to make
 in the margin or in a graphic organizer?
Do I have questions? Insights?
 Judgments? Criticisms?

▪ Picture
How do I visualize this?
What's the "movie" running in my head?
How would I describe this?

▪ Predict
What has happened so far?
What do I think will happen next?
What clues help me make this prediction?

After Reading

A number of strategies and activities are appropriate for after reading. These strategies help students review, analyze, and reflect on the selection and help them check their own understanding of what they have read. Many after-reading activities, such as completing exercises or summarizing, also provide a means for the teacher to assess students' understanding.

Facilitating the Jamestown Exercises

Jamestown reading series contain exercises after each selection that develop and improve reading comprehension and critical thinking skills. The QAR (question-answer relationship) strategy, taught in the minilesson on pages 39–41, will aid students in responding quickly and accurately to these exercises and to questions on standardized tests.

Extending Pre-reading Themes

The most effective post-reading activities extend the themes or reinforce the strategies that were introduced during pre-reading. Provide questions and activities specific to the selection that help students return to pre-reading activities. For example, have students review their purposes for reading and answer questions that were raised while activating prior knowledge.

Responding

After students have completed reading all or a key segment of text, it is important to have them respond, or react, to what they have read. Students might comment on the characters or the outcome of the plot. What did the main character learn? Should the main character have handled a situation differently? If so, how? By sharing their responses, students' involvement in the story deepens. The story becomes more meaningful, and students are more likely to retain what they have read.

After reading a nonfiction selection, ask students to comment on the ideas presented in the piece. What ideas were new to them? What surprised them? What confused them? What ideas would they like to know more about? After students have read persuasive pieces, ask whether they agree with the views presented. Have their views changed as a result? If so, how?

Summarizing

Besides serving as an assessment tool, summarizing improves students' reading comprehension and is an effective study skill. You may choose to have students summarize a selection independently, sharing their work afterward in a class discussion, or have the class develop a summary together by asking volunteers to contribute consecutive parts. (See pages 61–63 for the minilesson on Summarizing.)

> "The most important and basic response to a story involves the emotions."
> —Dianne Monson, "Characterization in Literature: Realistic and Historical Fiction." In *Children's Literature in the Reading Program*

Making Connections

Students comprehend a selection better when they make connections between the text and their own lives. Students can connect to the text by thinking about how ideas in the text relate to

- their personal experiences (text to self)
- other things they have read (text to text)
- the world they live in (text to world)

When students finish reading a selection, start a class discussion by posing questions or situations that are relevant to the core ideas, conflicts, or themes in the selection. As an alternative to discussion, you may ask students to respond by writing in a quickwrite format. Ideas for prompting student connections to texts are listed in the following chart.

Connections	Student Connections to Text	Sample Discussion or Quickwrite Topics
Text to Self	• Relate personal experiences that are relevant to selection themes or plot developments. • Make judgments or conclusions about characters or ideas in the text.	• *Discuss:* Do you agree with the author's position? Why or why not? • *Quickwrite:* Put yourself in the main character's place. Write a journal entry telling how you feel about events in the story.
Text to Text	• Determine how the ideas presented in an article would affect or interplay with ideas presented in another article. • Compare two texts in terms of their ideas, tone, impact, plot, or characters.	• *Discuss:* Compare similar factors (such as disasters) in the two articles. In your opinion, which one caused greater changes? Give your reasons. • *Quickwrite:* What might the character in text A advise the character in text B to do?
Text to World	• Decide how the ideas expressed in a text could affect the students' community. • Take an action based on information from an article.	• *Discuss:* How do you think people in our community would react to similar circumstances? • *Quickwrite:* Compose an ad for the school newspaper in which you promote your position on the issue.

Strategy Combinations

Following are three techniques, or instructional strategies, that can effectively guide your students' reading process. Each technique incorporates the use of several reading strategies and has an accompanying graphic organizer. Students use the graphic organizer at each stage of the reading lesson—before reading, during reading, and after reading.

KWL: Especially for Reading Nonfiction

KWL (What I *Know,* What I *Want* to Know, What I *Learned*) is a three-step instructional strategy used primarily with nonfiction texts. Students activate their prior knowledge, make predictions, read actively, summarize, and review key information as they complete a KWL graphic organizer. In the three-column KWL graphic organizer, students record information before, during, and after reading a selection.

Step 1: What I *Know* The purpose of step 1 is to engage students in thinking about the topic of the selection *before* they begin reading. Activate your students' prior knowledge by brainstorming with them about the topic. Ask leading questions that are relevant to the content of the selection. For example, for a selection about the plague, you might ask questions such as the following: What do you know about the plague? How was it spread? What were its symptoms?

Step 2: What I *Want* to Know Step 2 is also done in the pre-reading stage. First, have students preview the text. (For information on previewing, see page 15.) Then, building on the interest raised in step 1 and on the information students have gleaned from previewing, brainstorm with them to find out what they are curious to learn. Have students record what they want to know in the form of *questions* in the second column of the graphic organizer. Their questions will help provide them with purposes, or goals, for reading the selection.

Step 3: What I *Learned* Readers perform step 3 both during and after reading the selection. The purpose of step 3 is to have students identify key points from the reading, in particular those key points that the students did not know before reading. Students will record what they have learned—focusing on key information—in the third column of the KWL chart. Students should also seek answers, during and after reading, to the questions they framed in the second column. As students complete the third column of the KWL chart, encourage them first to fill in the information they recall from memory. Then have them skim back through the text to fill in key missing ideas.

Name _____

KWL Chart

Topic _____

Title _____

K	W	L
What I *Know*	What I *Want* to Know	What I *Learned*

SQ3R: For Reading Textbooks

SQ3R (**S**urvey-**Q**uestion-**R**ead-**R**ecite-**R**eview) is a five-step process that helps students read textbooks and other dense informational texts. It is an effective technique for reading any text that is organized into sections, especially expository texts with headings and subheadings.

The following page, which explains the five steps of SQ3R, can be copied and distributed to students as a study aid. With the class, read through each step of the technique in order. Model each step, using an informational selection. Then have students practice using each step of SQ3R until they can use the method independently.

Story Map: For Reading Fiction

As students read a fictional selection, have them complete a story map graphic organizer (see page 25). They will record information before, during, and after reading. Completing a story map can help students focus on text and identify and recall the main elements of fiction: characters, setting, and plot.

A story map graphic organizer helps students see the "bare bones" of a story as they chart the story's development. Completing a story map requires the student to not only gather information that is important for understanding the story, such as the characters' names, but also requires the student to think analytically. What is the problem in the story? How is that problem solved? Students must determine which events to list on the story map. Only those that are important or that may lead to a solution to the problem should be listed. From their story maps, students see that the plot events take place in a logical order. Events occur within the context of a setting—the time and place of a story. Often these events, or the lesson a character learns, lead the student to understand the story's theme, or deeper significance.

Before Reading Preview the story with students by guiding them to read the title and to look through the illustrations. Read aloud the first paragraph of the story. Then read enough of the story to enable students to identify the main characters, the setting, and the main story problem (the conflict). Ask students to fill in these elements in the graphic organizer.

During Reading Have students fill in the major events in the plot of the story. They also may add the names of any new characters as well as brief descriptions of the characters they have listed.

After Reading After students complete the reading, they should record on the story map the solution to the main problem in the story, revealing how the problem or conflict was resolved. The story map can then serve as a guide that helps students review and reflect on the story.

Name _____

SQ3R

Survey Complete this step *before* reading. It helps in two ways: (1) to get focused and (2) to build a framework for the text.	*Survey these things:* • Title • Headings and subheadings • Pictures, charts, illustrations, captions • Reading aids (for example, boldface terms and questions at the end of the selection) • Introductory and concluding notes
Question This step activates the brain for learning. (Repeat this step—plus the next two steps—for each reading segment.)	*Before you read the section, do these things:* • Turn the heading or subheading for the section into a question. • Write your questions on the left-hand side of a piece of paper.
Read Continue to read one section at a time.	*As you read the section, do these things:* • Look for the answer to your questions. Write the answers beside the questions. • Slow your reading speed for difficult parts. • Stop and reread parts that aren't clear. • Look for the main ideas.
Recite Complete this step after you read the section. It will help you to concentrate and learn while you read.	*After you read the section, do these things:* • Cover the answers you wrote. Answer the questions from memory. • If you can't remember the answers, reread the part of the section that has the answer. **Repeat Question-Read-Recite for each section of the text.**
Review Complete this step after you read the entire selection. It will help you to recall the information, because memory is strengthened through repetition.	*After you have read the entire text, do these things:* • Review all of your questions. Try to recite the answers from memory. • To find an answer that you cannot recall, reread the appropriate section of the chapter. Recite the answer. Then continue with the next question.

Name _____

Story Map

Title _____

Setting

Characters   _____   _____

_____   _____

_____   _____

Problem

Event 1 _____

Event 2 _____

Event 3 _____

Event 4 _____

Event 5 _____

Solution

Skills and Strategies Minilessons

The following minilessons can guide your teaching of key reading and vocabulary skills and strategies.

Monitoring Comprehension

1 Teach the Strategy

Explain how to monitor comprehension. Explain to students that monitoring comprehension means checking their own understanding of text as they read. An effective way to check understanding is by framing questions to themselves, based on the information provided in the selection. (Such questions might be: Who is this character? Why did the character act in this way? Why did the other characters respond as they did?) If students cannot answer their own questions, they need to find out where their understanding has broken down and use various techniques to aid their understanding of the text.

Introduce the "fix-up strategies." Explain that readers perform specific tasks to repair, or "fix up," their comprehension when it "breaks down." Review the fix-up strategies on the student handout on page 27.

2 Model

Model monitoring comprehension and using fix-up strategies. Read aloud a complex passage. As you read, pause to question information that your students may find confusing. For example, after reading a long, difficult sentence in a passage about Mount St. Helens, question specific points in the sentence. You might ask, "What do shock waves have to do with the eruption of Mount St. Helens? Do the shock waves somehow *cause* the eruption?" Then reread at a slower pace or read a sentence or two ahead to see whether the meaning of what was read becomes clearer. Demonstrate the use of each fix-up strategy on the student handout.

3 Provide Student Practice

Assign students to silently read a short selection, monitoring their own comprehension. Have them attach sticky notes with questions to the places in the text where they ask themselves questions or where they need help clarifying the meaning of the text. After they have finished reading, review as a class the reading problems that arose and have students suggest and model appropriate fix-up strategies.

Using Fix-Up Strategies

To Make Sure I Understand What I Read

1 **Stop.**

Notice when your understanding breaks down. When you lose the meaning, stop and fix the problem.

2 **Identify the problem.**

Ask yourself: "Where did I stop understanding the text? What is it that I don't understand? What is my question about the text?"

3 **Apply a Fix-Up Strategy. (see below)**

Reread.

Go back to the place where you lost the thread of meaning. Reread from there.

Read ahead.

Read on to clarify the meaning.

Alter the pace or voice.

Read more slowly. Try reading out loud.

Ask for help.

Ask a classmate or the teacher for help.

Fix-Up Word Strategies

1. Teach the Strategy

Introduce the fix-up word strategies. Point out that all readers come across words as they read that they do not know. Explain that readers use specific strategies to help them figure out the meaning of unfamiliar words. Call attention to the seven fix-up word strategies listed on the student handout or write the strategies on the board.

2. Model

Model how to use the fix-up word strategies. From a reading selection, locate a passage with a word that is unfamiliar to most students. Read up to the point where the word appears. Stop and model the first four strategies listed on the student handout. Note that each of the four steps should be completed quickly. (If readers labor over pronouncing a difficult word, they often lose the thread of meaning, and reading becomes tedious.) Then demonstrate how to use the next two fix-up strategies (reread and read on); both involve using context clues.

3. Provide Student Practice

Assign students to read a short selection silently and independently. Suggest that they attach sticky notes to words that are at first unknown. Have them list on each sticky note the fix-up strategies they used to understand the meaning of the word. After students have completed the reading, invite them to discuss the words they learned and the fix-up word strategies they used.

You may want to have students practice using the fix-up word strategies with several passages until they are comfortable using the strategies. During guided reading, think aloud as you use the strategies. Then have students think aloud as they use the fix-up strategies with other words.

Minilessons

Name _____

Using Fix-Up Word Strategies

To Understand Difficult Words

Sound out the word.   Use phonics (letter sounds) to pronounce the word.

Take the word apart.   Briefly examine the word parts. Find the root if you can. Take away the prefix. Take away the suffix.

Take a guess.   Pronounce the word as best you can. Any guess helps as you move on.

Read ahead to the end of the sentence.   Read the rest of the sentence and see whether your word makes sense.

Reread.   If your word guess does not make sense, reread the sentence and guess again. If you are close, the actual meaning of the word will become obvious.

Read on.   Read ahead. Often the meaning of the word becomes clear when you do this. NOTE: You may skip the word if you do not need it to understand the meaning of the text.

Seek help.   If the word is important and you cannot figure it out:
- Look it up in the dictionary—a sure thing.
- Ask someone who may know the word.

Context Clues

 Teach the Strategy

Explain the strategy. Write on the board the following words: *retractile, nocturnal, solitary, scarce, lairs, vocalizations, lionesses, zoologists, savannahs,* and *carcass.* Distribute copies of the student handout (pages 31–32), which includes the use of these words in sentences. Explain that all readers come across words they do not know. When this occurs, there are ways to figure out the meanings of most unfamiliar words. Explain that they should start by looking at the sentences around an unknown word. The nearby sentences are called the *context.* When students study the surrounding sentences to figure out the meaning of a new word, they are using *context clues.*

Read aloud with students the five-step strategy on using context clues on page 31. Then direct students' attention to the types of context clues listed on the student handout. Read aloud the first row, which describes comparison clues.

2 Model

Model the five-step process of using context clues. Use context clues to demonstrate unlocking the meaning of the word *retractile* in the first example on the student handout.

> **Think-aloud** I don't know what the word *retractile* means. I'll look for clues in the two sentences provided. The first sentence says that house cats can pull their claws into their paws. The next sentence states that tigers *also* have retractile claws. The clue *also* tells me that a tiger's claws must be like a house cat's. In other words, tigers must also be able to pull their claws into their paws. I think that *retractile claws* are claws that can be pulled in. Let me reread the sentence to see whether that definition makes sense: "House cats can pull their claws into their paws. Tigers also have *claws that they can pull in.*" Yes, the definition seems to fit.

3 Provide Student Practice

Guide students in using context clues. Have students work independently or in pairs to figure out the meaning of each underlined word in the Examples column of the chart. Ask students to highlight or circle the context clues that help them figure out the meaning of a word and have them write the meaning of each underlined word after the example sentence. Verify that students are using the five steps of the strategy and that they check to see that their guesses make sense in context.

Name _____

Using Context Clues

Follow these steps when you come across an unfamiliar word.

1. Read the words and sentences surrounding the unknown word. Look for the gist of the passage.

2. Ask: "What word would make sense in this context?"

3. Look for connections to the unknown word, such as comparisons, contrasts, definitions, or examples.

4. Guess at the meaning of the unknown word.

5. Test that meaning in the sentence. Does the sentence make sense with the new word or words?

Types of Context Clues

Read the information provided for each type of context clue. Then read the sentences in the Examples column. Use the context clues in each sentence to write a definition of the underlined word.

Types of Clues	Signal Words	Examples
Comparisons The context may contain a word or phrase that means nearly the same thing as the unknown word. When things are *compared,* similarities are shown.	*like* *similar to* *also* *in addition* *as* *related to*	1. House cats can pull in their claws. Tigers also have <u>retractile</u> claws. retractile _____ _____ 2. Like other <u>nocturnal</u> hunters, such as lions and leopards, tigers always wait until night to look for prey. nocturnal _____ _____
Contrasts The context may contain a word or phrase with an opposite meaning to the unfamiliar word. When things are *contrasted,* differences are shown.	*but* *however* *on the other hand* *unlike* *although* *despite*	3. Unlike lions who hunt as a group, tigers are <u>solitary</u> hunters. solitary _____ _____ 4. When their usual food sources are plentiful, tigers almost never attack human beings. However, when food is <u>scarce</u>, tiger attacks on people increase. scarce _____ _____

Name _____

Types of Clues	Signal Words	Examples
Examples Sometimes the context provides *examples* of an unknown word.	*for instance* *like* *such as* *especially* *this* *these*	5. A tiger has several <u>lairs</u>. *For example,* one lair might be in a rocky crevice near a waterfall. Another might be beneath some fallen trees. lairs _____ _____ 6. Tigers communicate through a wide range of <u>vocalizations</u>, *such as* roaring, growling, hissing, mewling, and grunting. vocalizations _____ _____
Definitions Context may directly explain the meaning of a new word.	Context may provide ● a definition in parentheses ( ) ● a definition separated by commas (,) or dashes (—) ● a definition following these signal words: *that is* *also known as* *also called* *which are* *in other words*	7. The swifter female lions (<u>lionesses</u>) do most of the work in a pride. lionesses _____ _____ 8. <u>Zoologists</u>, scientists who study animals, may observe wild cats in their natural habitats. zoologists _____ _____ 9. Tigers can be found in many Asian <u>savannahs</u>, which are grasslands containing few trees. savannahs _____ _____
General Context Sometimes clue words are not given. Then look for clues in the *gist* of the passage.		10. After making a kill, a tiger roars loudly. Then it drags the <u>carcass</u> near shade and water. There it takes two or three days to eat what it has killed, depending on the size of the carcass. carcass _____ _____

Below are sample student responses for the context sentences provided in the
Examples column of the student handout (pages 31–32).

Word	Context Clues	Meaning of Word
1. retractile	*Comparison:* House cats are compared to tigers. Both have claws that "pull in."	able to be pulled in
2. nocturnal	*Comparison:* night	occurring at night
3. solitary	*Contrast:* "as a group"	being the only one
4. scarce	*Contrast:* plentiful	opposite of a great deal; low in number
5. lairs	*Examples:* • rocky crevice • beneath fallen trees	resting or living places of wild animals
6. vocalizations	*Examples:* • growling • hissing • mewling • grunting	sounds made by an animal
7. lionesses	*Definition:* separated by parentheses	female lions
8. zoologists	*Definition:* separated by commas	scientists who study animals
9. savannahs	*Definition:* "which are"	grasslands containing few trees
10. carcass	*General Context:* Text talks about "a kill." Tiger drags it and eats it.	the body of a dead animal

Word Parts: Prefixes and Suffixes

① Teach the Strategy

Present a situation in which the strategy of recognizing word parts is called for. Write the word *disagreeable* on the board. Tell students that long words such as this can look hard when we first see them. Explain that such words are easier to read and understand when they are broken down into smaller parts. Write the following terms on the board and discuss their meanings:

prefix: word part at the beginning of a word
suffix: word part at the end of a word
root: the main part of a word to which a prefix or suffix, or both, can be added; when the root is a complete word, it is called a root word.

Tell students that recognizing common prefixes and suffixes, and knowing their meanings, can help readers unlock the meanings of thousands of new words.

② Model

Model the process of breaking a word into parts and analyzing meaning. Break *disagreeable* into parts on the board and label each part. Explain that the prefix *dis-* means "not" and that the suffix *-able* means "able to." Write students' suggestions for the meaning of the root word *agree*. (Be sure to record the meaning "to be in harmony.") Explain that by putting the word parts together, we learn that *disagree* means "not in harmony with" and that *disagreeable* means "not able to be in harmony with"—in other words, "unpleasant" or "offensive."

③ Provide Student Practice

Guide students in breaking words into parts. Write the following words on the board. Ask volunteers to identify the prefix, suffix, and root in each word. Then have them use the word parts as clues to help them guess the meaning of the entire word.

disconnection	dis connect (t)ion	state of not being connected
nonconformity	non conform ity	state of not conforming
disorderliness	dis orderli ness	state of not being orderly

Word Parts: Prefixes and Suffixes

Prefixes

Prefix	What It Means	Examples
1. in-	not	*insensitive* (not sensitive; lacking feeling)
2. im-	not	*immobile* (not mobile; fixed)
3. dis-	not; apart; opposite of	*disagree* ("not agree"; dissent) *dismantle* (take apart)
4. re-	again; back	*redundant* (same thing said again; repeated)
5. ex-	out of; from	*expel* (send out; drive out)
6. il-	not; without	*illogical* (not logical)
7. mal-	bad; badly inadequate; inadequately	*malnutrition* ("bad nourishment"; condition caused by insufficient nourishment)
8. bi-	two	*bisect* (cut in two)
9. post-	coming after; later	*postscript*, *"p.s."* (writing "after"; a note added after completing a letter)
10. sub-	under; beneath	*subway* (underground "way"; underground transport)
11. fore-	in front of; before	*forecast* (predict beforehand)
12. mis-	bad; wrong badly; wrongly	*misdiagnose* ("diagnose wrongly"; incorrectly identify a disease or condition) *misshapen* (shaped badly; deformed)

Suffixes

Suffix	What It Means	Examples
1. -able, -ible	able to; capable of	*washable* (capable of being washed; safe to wash without causing damage) *collectible* (can be collected; an item that can be collected)
2. -al	of; relating to; characterized by	*magical* (of magic)
3. -an, -or, -er	a person who; one who	*politician* (a person who is in politics) *conductor* (one who conducts)
4. -ful	full of; having; characterized by	*graceful* (full of grace) *respectful* (having respect; showing respect to others)
5. -fy	to make; to cause to be	*clarify* (to make clear)
6. -ion, -tion	state of being; act of	*fascination* (the state of intriguing or of being intrigued)
7. -less	without	*clueless* (without clues; lacking information needed for understanding)
8. -ness	state of being; quality of being	*darkness* (state of being dark)
9. -ment	state of being; act or process of	*empowerment* (state of being empowered)
10. -ous	having; characterized by	*malodorous* (having a bad odor)
11. -some	making one feel; having a feeling	*lonesome* (feeling lonely) *worrisome* (making one worry)
12. -ic	made of; relating to; having the qualities of	*metallic* (made of metal; resembling metal)

Predicting

1 Teach the Strategy

Present a situation in which predictions are made. Discuss with students the "mental game" of sports, pointing out that good athletes "keep their heads in the game." They look ahead and predict what other players will do in order to situate themselves in the best possible position for making plays or helping with the defense. Explain that looking ahead and making predictions serve the same function in reading as they do in sports. Readers "keep their heads in the game," think ahead, and anticipate what will happen next. Distribute the student handout on page 37, Predicting. Discuss the information in the chart.

2 Model

Model the strategy. Then distribute the student handout on page 38, the passage from the story, "The Horse of the Sword." Have students preview the selection, using the pertinent information in the Predicting chart. Ask them to predict what the story will be about. Then read aloud to the first bracketed stopping point in the story. Stop and model making predictions during reading by thinking aloud.

> **Think-aloud** The Flagman probably has a lot of experience with watching horse races. If he says that it is too late for MoroGlory to catch up to the other horses, I think he may be right. On the other hand, the rider seems to have a strategy. He holds back his horse at the beginning of the race, saying that he knows what "must be done." He shows confidence in MoroGlory by not accepting or being discouraged by the Flagman's comment. I think this horse has a lot of talent that isn't clear to others yet. I predict that the horse will move up in the race and that if he doesn't win, he'll come close.

3 Provide Student Practice

Guide students in making predictions. Call on a volunteer to read up to each bracketed stopping point. Ask students to jot down a prediction of what may happen, *as well as their reasons for making the prediction.* Invite students to share their predictions and reasoning. Then have students continue reading to the end of the story. After they have read, discuss students' predictions and how they verified the predictions or modified them after reading each section.

Name _____

Predicting

Make Predictions *Before* Reading
Get focused to read by skimming the selection.

Fiction	Nonfiction

Preview these parts:
• illustrations
• headnote
• beginning of the story
 	
Identify
• main characters and conflict
• setting
• tone of the story
  (Is the story funny?
  Is it serious?)
	Preview these parts:
	• headings, subheadings
	• illustrations, photos, captions
	• headnotes, summary paragraphs
	
	Look for
	• the topic of the selection
	• the author's purpose

Make Predictions *During* Reading
Stop frequently and make predictions about what is coming up.

Fiction	Nonfiction

Ask:
"What do I think may happen next?"
 	
Good stopping points:
• after a key event
• when the author hints or gives
  warning signs about future
  possibilities
	Ask:
	"What do I think the next passage is about?"
	
	Good stopping points:
	• at every heading or subheading
	• every three or four paragraphs

from "The Horse of the Sword"

by Manuel Buaken

A young man races his wild, "outlaw" horse, MoroGlory,
who bears the natural marking of a sword on his neck.

The starter gave his signal and the race began. Allahsan led out at a furious pace; the other horses set themselves to overtake him. It hurt my pride to eat the dust of all the others—all the way out the first mile. I knew it must be done. "Oomh, Easy," I commanded, and MoroGlory obeyed me as always. We were last, but MoroGlory ran that mile feather-light on his feet.

At the river's bank all the horses turned quickly to begin the fateful last mile. The Flagman said, "Too late, Boy," but I knew MoroGlory. **[PREDICT: Is the rider "too late"?]**

I loosened the grip I held and he spurted ahead in flying leaps. In a few space-eating strides he overtook the tiring Allahsan. The pacesetter was breathing in great gasps. "Where are your magic wings?" I jeered as we passed.

"Kiph," I urged MoroGlory. I had no whip. I spoke to my horse and knew he would do his best. I saw the other riders lashing their mounts. Only MoroGlory ran as he willed.

Oh, it was a thrill, the way MoroGlory sped along, flew along, his hooves hardly seeming to touch the ground. The wind whipped at my face and I yelled just for pleasure. MoroGlory thought I was commanding more speed and he gave it. He flattened himself closer to the ground as his long legs reached forward for more and more. Up, and up. Past the strong horses . . .

Now there was only Katarman, the black thunder horse ahead, but several lengths ahead. Could MoroGlory make up this handicap in this short distance, for we were at the Big Mango tree—this was the final quarter. **[PREDICT: Will MoroGlory catch up?]**

"Here it is, MoroGlory. This is the big test." I shouted. "Show Katarman how your Sword conquers him."

Oh, yes, MoroGlory could do it. And he did. He ran shoulder to shoulder with Katarman.

I saw that Katarman's rider was swinging his whip wide. I saw it came near to MoroGlory's head. I shouted to the man and the wind brought his answering curse at me. I must decide now—decide between MoroGlory's danger and the winning of the race. That whip might blind him. I knew no winning was worth that. I pulled against him, giving up the race. **[PREDICT: Will MoroGlory lose the race?]**

MoroGlory had always obeyed me. He always responded to my lightest touch. But this time my sharp pull at his bridle brought no response. He had the bit between his teeth. Whip or no whip, he would not break his stride. And so he pulled ahead of Katarman.

"MoroGlory—The Horse of the Sword," the crowd cheered as the gray horse swept past the judges, a winner by two lengths.

—from *Discoveries,* Five-Star Stories

QAR: Question-Answer Relationship

1 Teach the Strategy

Explain what the QAR strategy is. This strategy helps students answer questions about a text by helping them analyze the relationship between the question and the answer. Distribute copies of the handout on page 40. Discuss the four types of questions described in the chart. Explain to students that some answers are directly stated in a text (Right There). Some answers are stated in words that differ from the words of the question and may be located anywhere in the text (Think and Search). Some answers are implied; they are based on clues the author has provided (Author and Me). And some answers use the information in the text as a starting point for developing the reader's own ideas (On My Own). Point out that using the QAR strategy will help them answer questions by making clear the kind of information they are being asked to provide.

2 Provide Student Practice

Have students apply the strategy. Distribute the article on page 41. Have students silently read "Spiders" and the questions that follow it. Then call on a volunteer to read the article aloud. Guide students to answer each question, using the QAR strategy to identify the type of question and where in the article the information for each answer can be found. The answers to the questions are provided below.

Question Type	Answer
1. Right There	eight
2. Right There	arachnids
3. Author and Me	Tarantulas live only in warm climates; it gets too cold in Canada.
4. Think and Search	Some spiders do not make webs.
5. Author and Me	Tarantulas are not nearly as dangerous as rattlesnakes. The effects of a tarantula bite may be no more serious than a sting.
6. Author and Me	No, many spider mothers die before their babies hatch. The spiderlings are on their own.
7. On My Own	(Answers will vary.) People should not fear spiders. Most spiders are not poisonous, and they avoid people. Because they move so quickly, spiders tend to frighten people. However, for the most part, spiders are not interested in people, but only in trying to survive.

Analyzing the Question-Answer Relationship

Types of Questions	Where to Find the Answers
Right There	• You can find the answer in the book, usually in one sentence. • The wording of the answer in the text may be very much like the wording of the question. • Questions often begins with words that ask specific questions, such as *who, what, when, where, how much,* or *how many.* Example: Which liquid is heavier—oil or water?
Think and Search	• To find the answer, you need to read several sentences and combine the information. • Questions may begin with general instructions such as "Explain," "Summarize," "What caused," or "Compare." • The wording of the question and the answer differ. Example: Explain why oil floats on water.
Author and Me	• Answer these questions by making inferences. • Use what you know from your own experiences and prior reading to help you answer the question. • Use logical reasoning to expand on the information provided by the author. Example: What happens if you try to mix castor oil and water?
On My Own	• The answers to these questions are not in the book. • To answer them, you need to use your own knowledge and judgment. • The questions often involve the subject matter or the theme of the text. Example: Can you think of a way to make taking castor oil more pleasing?

Name _____

Spiders

A spider is a small, eight-legged animal. Spiders are best known for the silk they spin. They use this silk to catch insects. Even large animals cannot escape from the sticky silk. Many spiders make webs. They use these webs as traps. If you look at a web, you can see the patterns made by the spider.

Some spiders do not make webs. One kind of spider catches its prey by jumping onto an insect. Another spider uses its silk like a fishing line. It swings the line until it catches the insect. Then it reels up the line to eat its catch.

Spiders look like many of the insects they eat. But they are not insects. Spiders belong to a group called arachnids. All of these animals have eight legs. None of them have feelers. Mites and ticks belong in this family.

Spiders lay eggs. Some large spiders lay 2,000 eggs at a time. One small spider lays just one egg. Many spiders die after they lay their eggs. The spiderlings must learn to take care of themselves.

Many people are afraid of spiders, but only a few spiders can hurt human beings. In fact, spiders are very helpful. They get rid of many harmful pests.

A tarantula is one kind of spider. It is large and hairy. Tarantulas are found in many warm climates. People in the Southwest often see them. Once people thought that a tarantula's bite could give humans a terrible disease, but this is not true. Tarantulas found in the U.S. may have a stinging bite. However, the spider's bite causes no illness or permanent damage.

–Adapted from Timed Readings, *Book One*

1. How many legs does a spider have?
2. What is the name of the group that spiders belong to?
3. Why aren't tarantulas found in Canada?
4. Summarize the main idea of the second paragraph.
5. Without treatment, a person who is bitten by a rattlesnake can lose a limb or even die. Compare the danger of tarantulas with the danger of rattlesnakes.
6. Do spider parents teach their young how to spin webs? Explain your answer.
7. Do you think people should fear spiders? Why or why not?

Main Idea and Supporting Details

 Teach the Strategy

Introduce the concept. Discuss with students what a main idea is. Bring out that whenever we communicate with someone, we try to get across important points. Authors do the same thing in their writing. In order to understand what we read, we must be aware of the main ideas that the author presents.

Point out that main ideas may be *stated* or *implied.* Present the following tips for locating main ideas and supporting details.

Stated Main Ideas Look for a summary sentence that states the main idea of the paragraph. Stated main ideas are often found in the first or last sentence of a paragraph.

Implied Main Ideas If there is no summary sentence, figure out the main idea by searching for key facts or ideas. Ask yourself: "What is this paragraph about? What is the main purpose of the paragraph?" Then state the main idea in your own words.

Supporting Details After finding the main idea, look over the paragraph again. Find facts or ideas that are related to the main idea. These are called *supporting details.*

 Model

Use a graphic organizer. Distribute copies of the article on page 43, "Can Animals Predict Earthquakes?" Then draw on the board a blank Main-Ideas Map graphic organizer as found on page 44. Have students read aloud the first paragraph of the article. Then add the needed information to the graphic organizer as you think aloud about finding the main idea and supporting details in that paragraph.

Think-aloud Sometimes a paragraph contains a summary sentence that expresses the main idea. That doesn't seem to be the case here. The first sentence is about a catfish acting strangely before an earthquake. However, none of the other sentences are about catfish. Just about every sentence is about a different kind of animal. I notice, though, that most of the sentences have something in common: Almost every one tells how an animal acted strangely before an earthquake. That seems to be the gist of the paragraph. I can state the main idea in my own words this way: "Animals all over the world have acted strangely before an earthquake." *(Record the main idea as shown in the graphic organizer on page 44.)*

Name _____

Can Animals Predict Earthquakes?

For centuries the Japanese noted that catfish leapt madly about in their ponds before an earthquake struck. In 1835 a huge flock of screaming seabirds flew over the city of Concepción in Chile. Hours later an earthquake destroyed the city. Minutes before the terrible San Francisco quake of 1906, dogs ran howling through the streets. In 1963, just before an earthquake in Yugoslavia, the zoo animals cried out and charged at the bars of their cages.

Were these animals somehow aware that an earthquake was coming? Many Asian people have long believed that animals can sense earthquakes about to strike. Western scientists, however, usually thought that stories about animals acting strangely were just tall tales. Yet, in time, the huge number of these animal stories has impressed the scientists. In recent years, the experts have begun to take a second look. Now most scientists believe that animals can somehow sense when earthquakes are about to take place.

The event that changed the views of many scientists took place in northeastern China during the early 1970s. Chinese scientists, using an instrument called a seismograph (SIZE-muh-graff), began to measure a series of large shocks in the earth. The seismic signals increased sharply, so in 1974 the Chinese experts flatly predicted that a major earthquake would occur within two years.

Six months later, the animals in the area went "crazy." Snakes "turned suicidal" by climbing out of their cozy underground homes and freezing in the winter cold. Rats ran through the streets in broad daylight. Birds in cages flew wildly about. Chickens refused to enter their coops. In general, the animal kingdom went berserk. Within hours, northeastern China was hit by a series of minor earth tremors.

Chinese officials were now certain that a major earthquake was coming soon. They ordered the evacuation of Haicheng—a city of more than one million people. Within a few hours after the evacuation, a huge earthquake struck. It reduced the city to rubble. Countless lives were saved because the Chinese had listened to the warnings of the animals.

–Adapted from the Critical Reading Series, *Phenomena*

Now that I've identified the main idea, I'll return to the paragraph to find important details. The strange behavior of the animals seems important, but the dates and the names of the cities do not. I'll record the important supporting details. *(Record details as shown in the graphic organizer below.)*

 Provide Student Practice

Have students find the main idea and the supporting details of each of the remaining paragraphs in the passage. Record their ideas in the graphic organizer. (See sample answers in the graphic organizer.)

Main-Ideas Map

Main Idea 1
Animals all over the world have acted strangely before earthquakes.
Details
• Catfish leapt madly.
• Seabirds screamed.
• Dogs howled.
• Zoo animals charged at bars of their cages.

Main Idea 2
Now most scientists believe animals can sense earthquakes.
Details
• Many Asian people have long believed this.
• Western scientists scoffed until the number of stories impressed them.

Title
Can Animals Predict Earthquakes?

Main Idea 3
Events in 1970s China changed scientists' views
Details
• Chinese scientists measured large shocks in the earth.
• Experts predicted earthquake within 2 yrs.

Main Idea 4
Six months later, animals went "crazy" before earth tremors.
Details
• Snakes "turned suicidal."
• Rats ran through streets in daylight.
• Bird in cages flew about wildly.
• Chickens refused to go into their coops.

Main Idea 5
The Chinese saved lives by listening to the animals.
Details
• They ordered evacuation of city.
• Earthquake struck soon after.
• It reduced city to rubble.

A reproducible Main-Ideas Map graphic organizer is available on page 86.

The graphic organizers on this page show other ways of organizing and recording the main idea and supporting details of paragraphs. Teach students how to use one graphic organizer. Wait for mastery before advancing to another kind of graphic organizer.

Fishbone

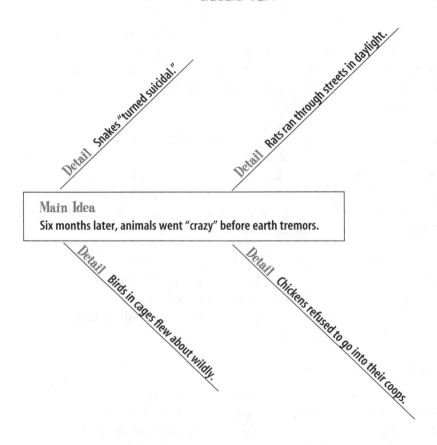

Main Idea and Supporting Details

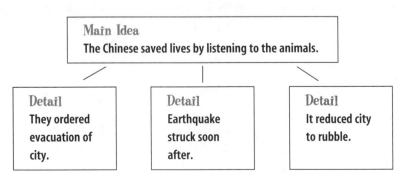

Text Structures

 Teach the Strategy

Explain why recognizing text structures is important. Tell students
that the principle underlying the study of text structures is that just
as stories follow a typical progression, informational texts are also
structured in a logical way. (A *structure* is the framework that the
writer has used to organize and present ideas.) When readers understand how a text is organized, they are prepared to read the text and
can better understand what they read. Unlocking the pattern of a text
gives readers an important tool.

Remind students that stories have a familiar text structure:
Characters move through a series of events called a *plot.* These
events take place in specific times and places, called the *setting.*
Explain that nonfiction texts also conform to predictable structures.
Unlike stories, which have one predictable structure, informational
text has several different patterns, or structures.

Tell students that four major text structures are Sequence,
Classification, Cause and Effect, and Comparison and Contrast.
Explain that authors often use more than one text structure in a piece
of nonfiction but that one overall text structure usually guides the
presentation of information.

 Lead a Class Discussion

Provide students with an overview of text structures. Distribute the
student handout on page 47, Understanding Text Structures: How
Information Is Organized. Tell students that they will be studying
each of these text structures in more detail so that they can recognize
them as they read. Read through the information in the chart. Discuss
the examples provided and ask students to supply additional examples of each text structure, referring to their own textbooks in various
subject areas.

Name _____

Understanding Text Structures

How Information Is Organized

Pattern of Text Structure	Description	Examples	Clue Words
Sequence (Time Order)	Lists events or steps in the order in which they occur in time	A nonfiction narrative, such as a biography, often presents events in the order in which they happened. A science book may describe the process of how a tornado forms.	*first* *next* *then* *finally* *last* *before* *later* *soon* *as* *meanwhile* *then*
Classification	Divides a topic into groups that share common characteristics	A science book may use a classification structure to describe the systems of the human body, such as *digestive, respiratory,* and *skeletal.*	*such as* *for example* *for instance* *specifically* *in particular* *in addition*
Cause and Effect	Shows the result of an event or situation or the reasons that it happened, or both	A science book may explain the conditions that *cause* an earthquake and the *effects* it produces.	*because* *since* *so* *as a result* *consequently* *therefore*
Comparison and Contrast	Compares two or more things, showing how they are alike or different, or both	A social studies book may describe the state of the country *before* and *after* the Civil War.	*however* *unlike* *by contrast* *in comparison* *although* *similar to* *different from*

Text Structure: Sequence (Time Order)

 Teach the Strategy

Define the sequential pattern of organization. Explain that when events are described in the order in which they occur in time or when information is told in a step-by-step manner, the text structure is said to follow sequence, or time order.

Identify the main types of sequential texts. The following two types of text are usually organized in sequence.

Narratives Tell students that a narrative is simply writing that tells a story. Point out that examples of nonfiction narratives include biographies and books about events in history. Most narratives present events in the exact order in which the events take place in time. (First, Helen Keller does not understand her teacher Annie Sullivan's actions of spelling words into her hand. Next, Annie Sullivan continues to spell the "names" of objects into Helen's hand despite Helen's resistance. Finally, Helen makes the connection between what she is touching—water—and the spelling Sullivan makes into her hand.)

Process/Directions Explain that informational materials some-times contain a process or procedure told step by step. For example, a science book may describe the process of how a tornado forms. (First, warm, moist air rises. Second, it collides with cool, dry air. Next, an anvil is formed.) Directions are also given in the order in which the steps should be completed.

Explain how to recognize sequential text structure. Ask students how they would recognize time-ordered, or sequential, text. (Events are told in the order in which they occur in time, or ordered steps are given.) Explain that signal words (such as *first, next, then),* dates, and clock times all help indicate time order.

 Model

Read aloud and then think aloud about the passage. Distribute the student handout on page 49, "'Don't Ride the Buses.'" Review with students the list of signal words for time order provided on the student handout. While students follow along, read aloud the first two paragraphs of the article. Then model identifying clues that may indicate the text structure.

Signal Words and Clues—Sequence			
first	last	as	dates
next	before	meanwhile	ages
then	later	then	seasons
finally	soon	during	time of day

"Don't Ride the Buses"

"We are asking every Negro to stay off the buses on Monday in protest of the arrest and trial [of Rosa Parks]. Don't ride the buses to work, to town, to school, or anywhere on Monday."

This statement was printed on 5,000 leaflets within 48 hours of the arrest of Rosa Parks in December 1955. Immediately it was distributed to black churches throughout Montgomery, Alabama. The leaflets told about Rosa Parks's arrest for refusing to move to the "colored section" in the back of a city bus.

On the first day of the boycott, African Americans looked for other means of transportation. They traveled by car, taxi, horse-drawn cart, mule, bicycle, and foot. They did not ride the buses.

Through the winter months, car pools were organized. Black-owned taxi companies also brought passengers to their destinations. The bus company's losses mounted. However, the owners refused to give in.

Meanwhile, lawyers for the boycott went to the federal court. They asked the court to rule against the unfair bus laws in Alabama. They won their case. The state of Alabama appealed to the U.S. Supreme Court. No one knew when the case would be settled.

In November 1956, the U.S. Supreme Court passed its ruling: Alabama's bus segregation laws were against the U.S. Constitution. After a year of boycotting, the 50,000 African American citizens of Montgomery had prevailed.

–Adapted from Six-Way Paragraphs in the Content Areas, *Middle Level*

Think-Aloud While reading the first paragraph, I can't tell where the quoted statement appeared or when. The writer doesn't give any time clues in the paragraph. When I read the second paragraph, though, the date jumps out at me immediately: December 1955. I also notice the phrase "within 48 hours of the arrest of Rosa Parks." Now I understand that the statement in the first paragraph was printed in a leaflet during December of 1955, 48 hours—two days—after Rosa Parks was arrested.

Suggest that students highlight or underline the clue words and phrases: "December 1955" and "within 48 hours."

3 Provide Student Practice

Have volunteers take turns reading the rest of the article aloud. Ask students to identify and mark signal words. ("first day of the boycott," "through the winter months," "meanwhile," "November 1956")

4 Introduce the Graphic Organizer: Flow Chart

Tell students that a flow chart is an effective way of showing the sequence of events or the steps presented in a time-ordered text. To demonstrate the use of the graphic organizer, draw a blank flow chart on the board and distribute copies of the Flow Chart graphic organizer (page 87). Work with students to identify key events in the article "Don't Ride the Buses." Record each main event in a separate box in the class graphic organizer as students follow along, completing their individual graphic organizers.

Flow Chart

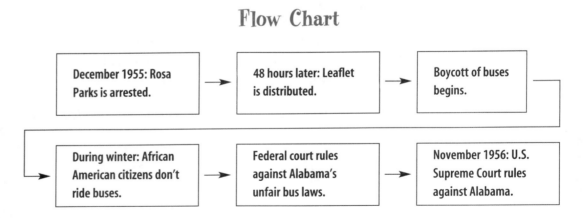

A reproducible Flow Chart graphic organizer is available on page 87.

Text Structure: Classification

① Teach the Strategy

Define the classification text structure. Explain that some nonfiction texts are organized by categories of information. For example, a science book may provide information about the human body by presenting sections on different systems of the body, such as one section on the digestive system and another section on the respiratory system. In turn, each main section may be subdivided into smaller sections. For example, the respiratory system may be subdivided into subsections on the nose, the windpipe, and the lungs. This kind of text structure is called *classification.* Illustrate the example in a graphic organizer on the board.

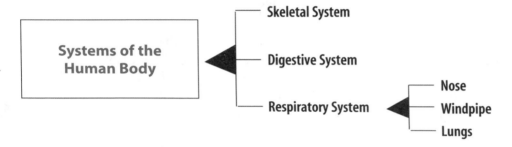

② Model

Demonstrate how to recognize the classification text structure. Distribute copies of the student handout on page 52, "Ready for High Speeds." To prepare students to recognize the classification text structure, call on volunteers to read the selection aloud. Then think aloud, calling attention to the following details:

Think-aloud As I started to read, I noticed that the article was about race car drivers. As I continued reading, I realized that the article was listing characteristics of a good race car driver. Signal words such as *also* and *another* helped me recognize this. For example, the beginning of the first paragraph says, "Drivers *also* have to be in good shape." And paragraph three says, "Good eyes are *another* 'must.'" The entire passage seems to be organized into a list of characteristics. Knowing that, I can reread the article and highlight the main classifications. Then I'll put the information into a graphic organizer that shows the main classes and how they are connected.

Ready for High Speeds

What kind of a person do you have to be to drive a race car? One thing you need is nerve—and plenty of it. At 250 miles per hour, a crash is never more than a split second away. You're driving a car that's being pushed to the limit. The engine is turning 10,000 times per minute, hour after hour. Most cars used for street driving would blow up if pushed past 7,000 turns per minute. The wheels, the clutch, or any part of the car could let go at any moment. But you stay composed and dive into the next turn.

Drivers also have to be in good shape. Excess body fat takes blood away from the brain and muscles. It also heats the body. In a hot race car, an overweight person would feel too warm. Fit race car drivers also need to be flexible. It is less likely that they will be hurt in a crash if their bodies can bend.

Good eyes are another "must." Drivers have to see things that are far away and be able to quickly judge how far away they are. They also have to see close-up things, like the oil gauge. Clear peripheral vision—the ability to see out of the corners of the eyes—is also important. Drivers need this kind of vision to see, for example, a wheel come off the car to the right.

Seeing objects ahead of time isn't enough. A driver has to decide what to do about what he or she sees—and do it—in an instant. How fast a person can act is called *reaction time.* Anyone who drives a car needs good reaction time, but in a race, a driver has to think much faster. Even 1/100 of a second can make a huge difference. At 200 miles per hour, that split second equals a whole car length!

–Adapted from *Reading Drills: Middle Level,* Edward B. Fry

3. Model Use of the Graphic Organizer

Draw on the board a blank version of the graphic organizer on page 51 and label it "Characteristics of a Race Car Driver." Reread aloud the first paragraph of the selection and suggest that the first quality needed is nerve. Insert the information in the graphic organizer.

4. Provide Student Practice

Guide students to supply the other main heads and subheads for the graphic organizer. Sample answers are shown below.

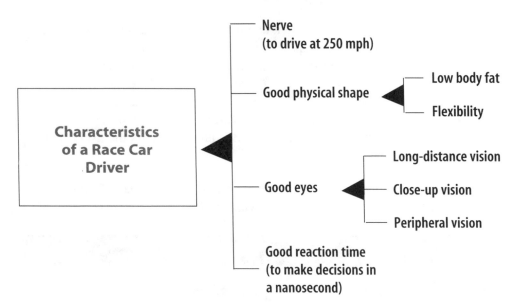

Text Structure: Cause and Effect

 Teach the Strategy

Introduce the cause-and-effect pattern. Remind students that a cause is the reason that something happens. It answers the question "Why?" An effect is a result of a cause or condition. Some nonfiction texts are patterned to explain either causes or effects, or both. For example, a newspaper article may describe the effects of a recent earthquake. A science book may explain the conditions that cause an earthquake.

Explain that one can recognize a text organized by cause-and-effect relationships by asking questions such as these: *Does the text discuss the reasons for an event? Does it discuss the effects that follow an event or situation? Does it answer or ask the question "Why?"* Tell students that clue words—such as *because, therefore, consequently, since,* and *as a result*—may signal a cause-and-effect pattern. Distribute the student handout on page 55, "A Malaria-Carrying Mosquito." Discuss the list of clue words on the handout.

Then explain that the cause-and-effect pattern can take many forms. Discuss the information in the following table.

Cause-and-Effect Pattern	Example or Explanation
One cause, one effect	Lack of rain caused a drought.
Several causes, one effect	Several events led to the school's closing.
One cause or condition, several effects	The tornado caused severe damage. Lives were lost. Homes were destroyed. Trees were uprooted.
A cause-and-effect chain	A cause leads to an effect that in turn becomes a cause that leads to another effect, and so on.

 Model

Model the strategy. Have a volunteer read the selection aloud. Then model analyzing the text structure as you think aloud.

A Malaria-Carrying Mosquito

First come the shakes, the fever, the burning throat. Next are the chills. Your pulse rate drops steeply, and a drenching sweat ices you from head to toe. Your face turns pale, and your nails turn blue. Then you either cough up thick, black blood and die—or you survive. These are the dreaded effects of the tropical disease *malaria.*

In 1904 the United States began building a canal through the Isthmus of Panama. Soon canal workers were getting sick; many were dying. That was because the hot, wet conditions in Panama were ideal for breeding the female *Anopheles*—a mosquito that carries malaria. These mosquitoes lay their eggs in standing water. The eggs can develop in rain barrels, storage jars, or puddles. Larvae, called *wrigglers,* hatch from the eggs and develop into adult mosquitoes. The adult mosquitoes feed on the blood of warm-blooded animals, including human beings. When the mosquitoes take in the blood of someone who has malaria, the deadly germs breed inside the mosquitoes' stomachs. Then the germs migrate to their mouth glands. After that, every person the mosquitoes bite gets a dose of the deadly disease. The cycle explodes. Infected victims give more malaria germs to other mosquitoes that bite them; these mosquitoes, in turn, infect more people. If left unchecked, cases of malaria can become epidemic.

Scientists were asked to determine how to stop the onrush of malaria in Panama. They advised getting rid of the standing water where the mosquito eggs were bred. Crews were sent to fill in swamps with dirt. They coated other watery areas with oil and larvicide. Certain fish, spiders, and lizards were put into rivers and fields to eat adult mosquitoes. Even human mosquito catchers were paid 10 cents an hour to swat the deadly insects.

Malaria was never wiped out entirely in Panama. However, it was greatly reduced. In 1906 some 82 percent of canal workers were infected with the disease. In 1913—the year that the canal was finished—less than 8 percent were infected.

–Adapted from Six-Way Paragraphs in the Content Areas, *Middle Level*

Think-aloud To find the text pattern for this selection, I'll start by rereading the first paragraph. *(Reread the first paragraph aloud.)* I first read the awful details—shakes, fever, burning throat—and I wonder what is *causing* them. The title of the article gives me a clue. When I read the last sentence of the first paragraph, I know for sure: Malaria is the *cause* of all of the *effects* described in the paragraph. To clarify this information, I will use a graphic organizer.

Draw on the board a Single Cause with Multiple Effects chart similar to the example shown below. Then continue with the think-aloud.

Think-aloud Malaria is the cause of all the effects listed in the first paragraph. I write this cause inside the main box of the graphic organizer. Since the paragraph includes information about symptoms at different stages of the disease, I'll list the effects by stage, one stage in each box. *(Create the First Stage effects cell of the chart.)*

3 Provide Student Practice

Guide students in supplying the details for the remaining "effects" cells.

Single Cause with Multiple Effects

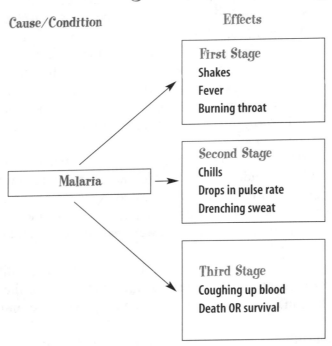

Cause/Condition

Effects

First Stage
Shakes
Fever
Burning throat

Malaria

Second Stage
Chills
Drops in pulse rate
Drenching sweat

Third Stage
Coughing up blood
Death OR survival

A reproducible Single Cause with Multiple Effects graphic organizer is available on page 88.

Minilessons

4 Model

Continue using the reading selection "A Malaria-Carrying Mosquito" to model a second variation in the strategy. Reread the second paragraph aloud and use details in a think-aloud to model recognizing sequential cause-and-effect relationships.

Think-aloud The first two sentences of this paragraph tell me that many Panama Canal builders were getting sick and dying in 1904. The clue word *because* in the third sentence lets me know that the writer is going to explain *why* the workers were getting sick. Reading on, I discover the following: *hot, wet conditions in Panama provided perfect breeding grounds for mosquitoes to lay their eggs in. The eggs developed into larvae that developed into adults. Some of the adult mosquitoes fed on the blood of people who had malaria. This, in turn, infected the mosquitoes.* I can see that a domino pattern is forming here: one cause leads to an effect. That effect, in turn, leads to another effect, which causes another effect, and so on.

On the board draw the graphic organizer shown below and fill in the first boxes with details provided by the class.

5 Provide Student Practice

In a guided discussion, have students supply the details for the remaining boxes in the Cause-and-Effect Chain graphic organizer.

Cause-and-Effect Chain

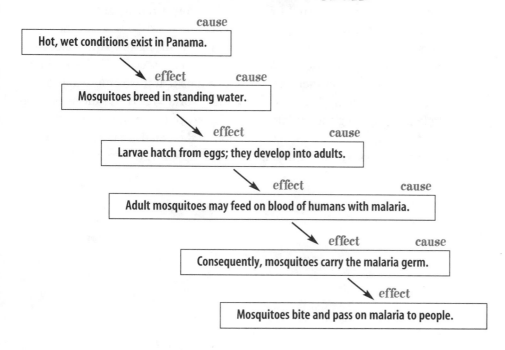

A reproducible Cause-and-Effect Chain graphic organizer is available on page 89.

Text Structure: Comparison and Contrast

1 Teach the Strategy

Describe a comparison-contrast pattern. Explain that some nonfiction texts compare two or more things, showing how they are alike and different. For example, a newspaper article about homerun hitters might compare the styles of Barry Bonds, Mark McGuire, and Sammy Sosa. Explain that noticing whether the text discusses similarities or differences between two or more people or things will help them recognize a comparison/contrast pattern. In addition, clue words such as *however, but,* and *nonetheless* signal differences, and clue words such as *similarly, in common,* and *same* signal similarities. Distribute the student handout "The Changing Middle Class" (page 59) and discuss the list of clue words provided on the handout.

2 Model

Model the strategy, using the reading selection. Call on volunteers to read aloud "The Changing Middle Class." Then use a think-aloud to call attention to the following details:

Think-aloud How do I know that two things are being compared in this text? The title of the article gives me my first clue. It indicates that the article is about "the changing middle class." The title leads me to predict that the writer will explain what the middle class used to be like and what it is like now. The first four sentences confirm my prediction. *(Read the first four sentences aloud.)* The clue word *however* in the second sentence signals to me that the writer is discussing differences. The first sentence mentions that the United States sees itself as a middle-class nation today, but then the article explains that it was more appropriate to use the term *middle class* right after World War II. It's clear that the article is comparing the middle class of today to the middle class after World War II. I will pay special attention to the details that describe what the middle class was like after that war and how it is different today.

Signal Words for Comparison/Contrast		
however	yet	same
but	in comparison	different from
unlike	although	in common
by contrast	similar to	shared

The Changing Middle Class

The United States sees itself as a middle-class nation. However, the middle class label does not fit in the same way as it once did. Being "middle-class" is more of a way of thinking about oneself than a fact. The term *middle class* was probably as true for this nation as it ever could be right after World War II. The economy was growing. More and more people owned their own homes. Workers had solid contracts with the companies that hired them. More people than ever before, if they wanted one, could have a college education.

The middle class has always held several values in common. Those values persist today. One strong value is the desire to earn enough money to control one's own economic future. In addition, the middle class commonly believes in certain morals. For example, members of this class embrace such ideas as the need for individual responsibility and the importance of family, obligations to others, and belief in something outside oneself.

However, in the 1990s those in the middle class found that there was a greater price to pay for success. A *U.S. News & World Report* survey in 1994 concluded that 75 percent of Americans believed that middle-class families could no longer make ends meet on a single salary. Both spouses now had to work: A sole wage earner could often not afford to raise a family in the desired lifestyle. Long commutes to work had become routine. The need for child care put strains on the family. Public schools were often not as good as they once were. In addition, members of the middle class were no longer financing their lifestyles through earnings; they were using credit to stay afloat. The understanding of just what *middle class* meant was changing.

–Adapted from Six-Way Paragraphs in the Content Areas, *Middle Level*

Model Use of the Graphic Organizer

Present a Venn diagram. Explain that comparison and contrast can be represented in a Venn diagram graphic organizer. Draw a Venn diagram on the board. If students need practice in using a Venn diagram, model its use by having students analyze the differences between two pieces of fruit, an apple and an orange. Label the left-hand circle *Apple;* the right-hand circle *Orange;* and the overlap between the circles *Both.* Record students' suggestions of attributes and characteristics unique to each piece of fruit in the designated circles and those shared by both types of fruit in the section labeled *Both.* (Sample responses: *Apple*—red or yellow; can be used in pastry; ripens in fall. *Orange*—color is orange; used to make juice; a flavor used in many products; must be peeled before eating. *Both*—fruit; usually sweet; common in U.S.; can be adapted to several uses.)

Draw another Venn diagram on the board and distribute copies of the Venn Diagram graphic organizer to students (see page 90). Ask students to record information on their individual Venn diagrams as the you complete the class diagram. Label the left-hand circle *Middle Class After World War II* and the right-hand circle *Recent Middle Class.* Label the overlapping section *Both.* Read aloud the first paragraph of the selection again. List details that describe the middle class after World War II in the left-hand circle of the Venn diagram. (See the model at the bottom of this page.)

 Provide Student Practice

Guide students in supplying the details for the middle and right-hand sections of the Venn diagram.

Venn Diagram

Middle Class after World War II
- More people owned their own homes.
- Workers had solid contracts with companies.
- More people could have higher education.

Both
Share common values:
- able to determine one's own economic future
- individual responsibility
- importance of family
- obligations to others
- belief in something outside oneself

Recent Middle Class
- cannot make ends meet
- both spouses need to work
- have long commutes
- need child care
- find public schools not as good
- use more credit

A reproducible Venn Diagram graphic organizer is available on page 90.

Minilessons

Summarizing

1 Teach the Strategy

Present the strategy and its purpose. Provide students with an example of summarizing from everyday life. Explain that if a student wanted to tell a group of friends about a party that he or she had attended, the student would not provide every detail of what had happened at the party. Instead, the student would relate the *main points* about the party—the special people who attended, one or two interesting incidents, and the main activities. In other words, the student would *summarize* what occurred at the party. Explain that summarizing a text is like summarizing the events at a party: it requires that you identify the main points and describe them in your own words.

Tell students that summarizing improves understanding of a text because it requires that the reader look for, organize, and explain key ideas. Summarizing is also a helpful memory aid. Then present the following steps for summarizing:

- Identify the topic of the whole piece and the key ideas of each paragraph. Clue: Look for words that are repeated.
- Underline or highlight the key ideas. These ideas will be the building blocks of your summary.
- Put the key points of the text in your own words. Omit the details.

2 Model

Model using the strategy. Distribute copies of the student handout on page 62, "Dogs That 'Think.'" Read aloud the first paragraph, stopping at the subhead "The Right Stuff." Then think aloud as you summarize, starting by identifying the key ideas.

> **Think-aloud** This seems to be a good place to stop and summarize what I've read so far. I'll begin by suggesting the topic of the whole piece. The first sentence reads, "Many dogs serve only as pets, but some dogs have jobs to do." I think this will be the topic of the whole piece.
>
> The first paragraph goes on to tell more about dogs that work. The paragraph explains what types of work dogs may do and that German shepherds are an excellent breed of working dog. I think the key idea of the paragraph is expressed as part of the first sentence: "Some dogs have jobs to do." I will highlight that part of the sentence.

> ## To Summarize a Text
> Explain the main points.
> Make it simpler.
> Make it shorter.
> Use your own words.

Dogs That "Think"

Many dogs serve only as pets, but some dogs have jobs to do. For example, they may work as police dogs or as guide dogs for the blind. Some breeds of dog do these jobs better than others. One of the best breeds of working dogs is the German shepherd.

The Right Stuff

German shepherds have many qualities that make them good work dogs. For one thing, they are the right size—large and strong. Their chests are big enough for getting plenty of wind for long runs.

The thick fur coat of German shepherds is another plus. Their coat protects them in bad weather when they need to work outside. It also helps them stay clean.

German shepherds are also very smart. It is easy to train them to do hard jobs. Working for the police, a German shepherd may have to sniff out drugs or follow faint tracks. Working for the blind, the dog may need to "read" traffic lights. German shepherds are smart enough to learn skills like these quickly and well.

What's more, German shepherds are patient and calm. If their owners are busy, they will not be jumpy or demand attention. They can wait quietly for a long time.

Poor Choices

Some dog breeds are not well suited for work. The dachshund is one example. It is too short and small for many jobs, and it is not very strong. In addition, a dachshund is not easy to train. Although smart, it avoids doing things it does not want to do.

Another poor choice is a poodle, even though poodles may be smarter than German shepherds. Poodles can be trained faster than shepherds can be, but poodles do not have good judgment. If a poodle led a blind person, it would do everything the person said. When that person said "Forward," the poodle would go forward, even if a car were coming! German shepherds, on the other hand know when *not* to follow an order.

–Adapted from Signature Reading, *D*

Now I'll read the section under the subhead "The Right Stuff." *(Read aloud the section titled "The Right Stuff.")* The paragraphs under this subhead are all about German shepherd dogs. They tell *why* German shepherds make good working dogs. The first paragraph in this section says that German shepherds are of a good size. I'll highlight the second sentence as a key idea. *(Highlight "They are the right size—large and strong.")*

Help students identify the key ideas in the remaining paragraphs in the first subheaded section. After the key ideas are identified, work with the class to create a summary, such as the following, of the first subheaded section:

> **Summary** For several reasons, German shepherds can be considered good working dogs. They are large and strong, with thick fur coats that protect them when they work outside. They are smart. Finally, these dogs are by nature patient and even-tempered.

③ Provide Student Practice

Ask students to summarize the second subheaded section, "Poor Choices." Have them identify the key ideas of each paragraph and then use the ideas to help them summarize the passage. (Sample summary: Some dog breeds are not good working dogs. The dachshund is small and difficult to train. The poodle, though smart, lacks judgment.)

Visualizing

 Teach the Strategy

Introduce the strategy of visualizing. The reading strategy of visualizing helps readers to enjoy a text and also to remember important information. Explain to students that visualizing is like taking a "mental photo" of what is described in a text. Readers use the details they read, as well as their own imaginations, to picture what is being described. Picturing a scene will help them understand what they read, as well as remember it.

Tell students that in narrative texts, readers might look for *sensory details*—details that appeal to the senses—in order to more fully picture a scene. Explain that visualizing is also a useful tool for reading informational texts. For example, readers will better understand the directions for building a model airplane if they picture each step. When students picture what they read about in their subject-area textbooks—such as a landing on the Moon or the swirling winds and green sky as a tornado forms—they are more likely to understand the information and to remember what they have read.

 Model

Model using the visualizing strategy. Distribute copies of the student hand-out on page 65, "Boston's Great Molasses Flood." Begin by reading aloud the *second paragraph* of the reading selection. Then present the following think-aloud.

> **Think-aloud** I'm picturing that enormous metal tank filled with warm molasses. The text says that the tank was 50 feet tall. That's about 5 stories high! And it was as big around as a football field. I know how big a football field is, so I can picture how huge that tank was!

 Provide Student Practice

Call on volunteers to read the rest of the passage aloud. Have students stop after each paragraph or description to share what they picture. Have them identify details in the text that helped create the images they have in their minds.

Boston's Great Molasses Flood

Molasses is a thick, sticky, sugar syrup that moves very slowly when it is poured. The colder it is, the more slowly it moves. But on January 15, 1919, molasses moved so fast that it snuffed out the lives of 21 people and wrecked a large part of Boston's North End.

In 1919 Boston's molasses was stored in a huge metal tank. The tank was 50 feet tall and almost 300 feet around—the length of a football field. Inside the tank were steam pipes that kept the molasses warm. On January 12, the tank was filled beyond what it should have been.

January 15 was an unusually warm day in Boston. At midday people were outdoors enjoying the sunshine. Workers from warehouses were outside on loading docks eating lunch, and many of the shopkeepers and residents were standing in doorways.

Suddenly a deep rumble shattered the warm day. Then there was a series of loud explosions. The molasses tank had burst open! A flood of steaming hot liquid gushed out of it. Molasses poured down Commercial Street. People in its path couldn't run fast enough to avoid it. The sticky sludge caught their feet and swirled the people around. Others scrambled to keep ahead of the sticky, hot wave. But it was 30 feet high! Twenty-seven million pounds of the sticky goo poured over walkers, lunch crowds, and workers. It overran buildings, lifting some right off the ground. Twenty-one people were either crushed by the mess or drowned in it.

Although there were cars and trucks back in the year 1919, most freight was still hauled by horses and wagons. Dozens of carts and horses became trapped in the sticky sludge. Horses reared and snorted. They rolled their eyes in fear as they found themselves unable to move in the ooze. Many of them fell over and suffocated. Police had to shoot some of the beasts that were trapped.

Many bystanders who tried to help the trapped victims soon found themselves caught knee-deep in sticky molasses. The stuff was worse than quicksand. Rescuers had to cut people right out of their clothes in order to free them. The clothes had become encrusted with a hard, sugary substance.

As weary folks slowly returned to their homes, they spread the molasses all over the city. The next day every city bench in the area was sticky. Molasses covered buses, trees, roofs, and overhead wires. The cleanup went on for days. Even after the injured had been cared for and the dead had been buried, Boston continued to live a nightmare. It was weeks before the odor of molasses disappeared. And the waters of Boston Harbor had a brown cast for months afterward.

–Adapted from the Critical Reading Series, *Disasters*

Reading with Jamestown

The following pages outline ideas and strategies for the teaching of reading that are specific to individual Jamestown series.

Critical Reading and The Wild Side

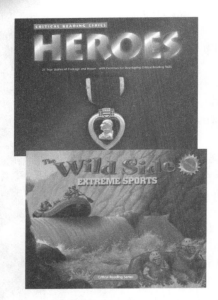

The Critical Reading Series (reading levels 6 to 8) including The Wild Side (reading levels 4 to 6) offers high-interest nonfiction articles and exercises to develop reading comprehension and critical thinking skills. The articles in both series present information about amazing, strange, or unbelievable events that students will want to read about. The exercises help students find the main idea, recall facts, make inferences, summarize and paraphrase, develop vocabulary, understand the author's technique, and apply critical thinking skills.

➡ **Before Reading** Have students preview the article they will read, noticing the title, the illustration, the caption, and any words that stand out to them. Next, have them read the first and last paragraphs. Then ask them to predict, on the basis of their preview of the article, what the article may be about. Build background knowledge by discussing what students know about the topic. To stir students' interest and to focus their attention on key ideas, ask them to complete, in pencil, the Reading Comprehension exercises (A, B, C, and D) that follow the article, either individually or with partners.

➡ **During Reading** Plan on having students read the article twice. (For suggested reading arrangements, see page 16.)

➡ **After Reading** Consider having students complete a Main-Ideas Map graphic organizer (page 86). Have students redo their answers to the Reading Comprehension exercises, in ink. Initiate a class discussion of the new information they received from their reading that caused them to change answers. After a second reading, have students complete the Critical Thinking exercises and the self-assessment items. Encourage students to explain the reasoning behind their answers and to elaborate on any reading strategies they applied.

Extending To help students increase their reading speed and accuracy, you may choose to time their reading of an article, as suggested in the *Teacher Notes and Answer Keys* for both Critical Reading and The Wild Side. Charts for recording student progress are provided at the end of each unit.

Critical Reading and The Wild Side

- high-interest nonfiction
- reading levels 4 to 8
- self-assessment, self-scoring
- timed readings

Five-Star Stories

The Five-Star Stories series includes 18 anthologies on 10 reading levels. These collections of high-interest short stories from around the world provide stimulating experiences with classic literature. The exercises focus on reading comprehension, critical thinking, vocabulary, and writing. The accompanying Five-Star Activity Books series provides additional fiction and nonfiction selections, as well as test-taking practice and extended writing activities.

When introducing the Five-Star Stories collections, begin by reading and discussing with the class the To the Student and the Literary Terms sections at the beginning of each book.

➡ **Before Reading** You may wish to have students preview the story, including reading the title and studying the illustration. Ask students to predict what the story may be about. Suggest that they begin a graphic organizer such as the Story Map (page 25) or the Flow Chart (page 87) to help them identify key elements in the story. If you are using level A or B of the series, discuss the vocabulary words with the students. Have volunteers use each word in a sentence.

➡ **During Reading** Have students read the story silently and ask them to add information to their story maps as they read. Then have students in small groups take turns reading orally. After each student reads, have other members of the group summarize what was read. This oral reading will provide opportunities for you and your students to model the process of monitoring comprehension and applying fix-up strategies. At the end of the story, ask group members to share their story maps and to summarize the entire story.

➡ **After Reading** Have students work independently to complete the exercises, check their answers, and calculate and record their scores. Scoring instructions and suggestions are included in the Five-Star Stories *Teacher Notes and Answer Keys* booklet. You may wish to have students discuss their answers with a partner or in a group.

Extending The extension activity at the end of each lesson offers opportunities for thoughtful class discussions and interesting writing assignments. These questions can be used as individual assignments or as group projects. The Five-Star Activity Books can also be used to extend learning and reinforce the skills taught in a lesson.

Five-Star Stories

- high-interest fiction
- reading levels 1 to 10
- adapted, abridged classic literature
- scoring graph and progress chart

Signature Reading

Jamestown's Signature Reading is a complete reading program that emphasizes strategy building and provides sequential development of comprehension and vocabulary skills. Each lesson provides a reading selection and before-, during-, and after-reading activities. Students learn how, why, and when to apply specific reading strategies. The exercises accompanying each lesson check students' comprehension of the selection as well as their vocabulary development and strategy use. Students graph their scores on the exercises to track their own progress in reading.

Signature Reading

- interactive reading
- reading levels 2 to 12
- fiction, nonfiction
- reading skills and strategies
- comprehension, vocabulary
- self-assessment, self-scoring

➡ **Before Reading** Refer to the *Annotated Teacher's Edition* and the teaching note for each selection found in the "T" pages of the book. Complete the pre-reading activities (including any graphic organizers) suggested in the Signature Reading lesson. Introduce the strategy that will be developed during reading.

 If your students would benefit from additional vocabulary practice, have them complete a word-sorting activity. Individually or in pairs, students should list in categories the vocabulary words from the lesson in Signature Reading and then should decide on labels for the categories. Ask students to watch for the vocabulary words as they read. Then have them decide, after reading, whether the categories they chose still make sense.

➡ **During Reading** Students might read in small groups or as a whole-class activity. (See additional reading options on page 16.) It is important to pause during reading to complete the Strategy Break activity.

➡ **After Reading** Work with students to follow up on the reading strategy. Then have students complete the exercises. If students have completed the word-sorting activity, have them reevaluate the categories they created for the vocabulary words. Discuss together ways they might like to recategorize the words. After students are satisfied with the categories they have created, ask them to write sentences for the words in each category. You might challenge students to write sentences that each contain two or more of the vocabulary words they have listed for a category.

Extending See the activities for extending the lesson provided in Signature Reading. For additional practice in reading, students might reread the selection in the format of readers theater or radio reading. Allow at least ten minutes for students to practice reading their parts before the group begins to read aloud.

Best Series

The Best series—*Best Short Stories, Best Nonfiction, Best Poems, Best-Selling Chapters,* and *Best Plays*—each provides an in-depth look at a specific genre of literature. Instruction is tailored to the specific attributes of the genre. For example, *Best Short Stories* provides lessons on story elements. *Best Nonfiction* provides lessons on reading skills especially useful for nonfiction reading, such as understanding the author's purpose. *Best Poems* provides lessons on poetic elements. Students utilize reading skills and strategies as they complete the exercises following each selection. Interesting and detailed writing assignments are provided.

➡ **Before Reading** Help students prepare to read by first reading together any introductory notes that precede the selection. Invite students to comment on illustrations, if provided. Ask them to scan the selection and then to use the title, illustrations, and information from the introduction and their scanning to help them predict what the piece will be about. Discuss students' predictions and their reasons for making them. Have students set a purpose for reading the selection.

➡ **During Reading** Students may read the selections in a variety of ways. (See page 16.) Choral reading is an effective way to present poetry. Drama comes vividly to life when presented as readers theater. Radio reading, which includes practice time before students read aloud and comprehension questions following each student's oral reading, might work especially well with nonfiction texts.

➡ **After Reading** In whole-class discussion, ask students whether their predictions about the content of the piece were correct. If not, how did the content differ from what they expected? Then have students meet in literature groups to discuss their responses to the selection. Members of groups may work together to create an oral summary of the piece.

Ask students to complete the exercises following the selection and to record their scores in charts, when provided. At future class meetings, teach the lesson that follows the selection and have students complete the related exercises and writing assignments. Lead the class in a discussion of the selection, using the discussion prompts provided in the book. Have students complete the final writing assignment at the end of the unit.

Extending Have students present all or a part of a literary piece to a partner, a small group, or the whole class. Students should practice before presenting their piece in order to read fluently and with appropriate pace and expression.

Best Series

- outstanding literature
- variety of genres
- reading levels 5 to 12
- reading skills and strategies
- writing assignments

Reading with Jamestown

Jamestown's Reading Improvement Series

Jamestown's Reading Improvement series includes *Reading Drills, Vocabulary Drills,* and *Skimming and Scanning. Reading Drills* lessons feature classic and contemporary fiction and nonfiction readings. The reading passages can help students increase their reading speed. *Vocabulary Drills* lessons help students acquire many new vocabulary words and also provide techniques for discovering the meanings of words encountered while reading. *Skimming and Scanning* lessons provide practice in using two key reading techniques (skimming and scanning) in various reading contexts.

➡ **Before Reading** For *Reading Drills,* have students read the introductory statement before each reading selection to prepare themselves to read. Explain the procedure for timing readings that will be used in your classroom. (You may wish to have individuals time themselves, using a stopwatch; or you may appoint a "timer" who is to record *1:00* on the board after students have read for one minute and then update that time every 10 seconds.) For *Vocabulary Drills,* review together the directions for completing the lesson. If students are to read a selection, encourage them to pay particular attention to boldfaced words. For *Skimming and Scanning,* review with students the process of skimming or scanning and other tips for applying the strategy as they appear in the "To the Student" section.

➡ **During Reading** The selections in all three series are meant to be read silently and independently. In *Reading Drills,* have students complete a timed reading.

➡ **After Reading** Ask students to complete the exercises provided and, if appropriate, to record their scores on the graphs and charts provided in their books. For *Reading Drills,* in addition, have students discuss their answers. Then have them complete the Personal Response question, at the end of each lesson, with a partner or in a small group. For *Vocabulary Drills,* provide opportunities for students to discuss their reasoning as they complete the exercises.

Extending For *Reading Drills,* have partners take turns retelling the key events in the selection. For *Vocabulary Drills,* students might utilize word grids (page 4) to explore more fully two words from the lesson. For *Skimming and Scanning,* encourage students to practice skimming and scanning authentic texts, such as newspapers or flyers.

Jamestown's Reading Improvement

- graduated levels
- reading levels 4 to 10
- strategic approach
- targeted exercises
- progress graphs, charts, or lists

Timed Readings

The Timed Readings series—*Timed Readings, Timed Readings in Literature, Timed Readings Plus, Timed Readings Plus in Science,* and *Timed Readings Plus in Social Studies*—provides passages of uniform length that are designed for systematic classroom practice to improve reading rate and comprehension of text. All of the Timed Readings include comprehension questions. Timed Readings Plus lessons contain two passages and include additional comprehension questions that call on students to use several specific reading skills and strategies. Progress graphs at the back of each book help students track their progress in improving reading speed and comprehension.

➡ **Before Reading** Explain to students that being aware of the type of material they will read will help them know what to expect and how to read the text efficiently. For example, when preparing to read a selection from *Timed Readings in Literature,* students might expect to find characters and connections between the related events in a story plot. Review the process of previewing before students use the books for the first time. (They should read the title, the first sentence, and the last sentence, and then should skim the selection.) After the first session, allow 20–30 seconds for students to preview a selection before reading.

➡ **During Reading** Stress to students the importance of focus and concentration during reading. Students may time themselves individually with a stopwatch, or a "timer" may be designated who will write *1:00* on the board after one minute has passed and update that time every 10 seconds. Students are to record the time it took them to finish reading the passage, marking the bottom of the page containing the passage.

➡ **After Reading** Have students complete the exercises and record their scores on the progress graphs at the back of their books. Encourage students to share in a whole-class discussion the strategies they used to read quickly and improve their comprehension.

Extending Have students complete a writing assignment, using information presented in the reading they have just completed. In response to a non-fiction reading, students might write a letter to the editor expressing their views about the subject matter. Alternatively, students might write interview questions for a person featured in the article. In response to a fiction reading, students might write a "what-if" story, exploring what might happen next to the characters in the selection. See page 7 for additional ideas for writing assignments.

Timed Readings Series

- timed selections
- reading levels 4 to 13
- reading rate
- comprehension exercises
- progress graphs

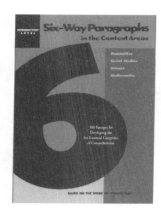

Six-Way Paragraphs

Six-Way Paragraphs (levels 1 to 12) and Six-Way Paragraphs in the Content Areas (levels 4 to 12) are designed to increase students' understanding and enjoyment of nonfiction writing. By reading the selections and completing the exercises that follow, students will strengthen their reading skills, especially those that aid comprehension of expository text. Six-Way Paragraphs in the Content Areas teaches students the essential skills and techniques needed to understand information and to apply the knowledge gleaned from text.

➡ **Before Reading** Have students preview the selection, noting the title and any words that stand out to them as they look over the passage. Consider having students read the first sentence of each paragraph as part of their previewing. (In addition, for Six-Way Paragraphs in the Content Areas, students should note the symbol that indicates the type of selection they will read—humanities, social studies, science, or mathematics.) Before students begin reading, you may wish to review a reading skills minilesson— particularly the minilesson, provided in this guide, on recognizing main ideas and supporting details. For focused practice of this skill, create a transparency of a passage from the book and display it on the overhead projector. Guide students to recognize stated and unstated main ideas and to distinguish between main ideas and supporting details.

➡ **During Reading** Ask students to read the selection and then to read quickly the questions following the selection, putting a pencil dot next to their answers to the questions. Then have students reread the passage slowly and carefully. Ask them to return to their questions and this time answer the questions carefully.

➡ **After Reading** Review the exercises in class. Tell students to record their scores and to graph their progress on the diagnostic charts and progress graphs at the back of the book. For additional practice, have students write another question for each of the question categories provided. In small groups, students can read aloud, discuss, and answer the additional questions. As a whole-class activity, have students suggest questions that go beyond the text they have read. What else would they like to know about the topic? How would they find that information?

Extending As a partner activity, have each student select two words that may have made understanding the selection difficult. Students then take turns following this procedure: One student states a word from the passage. The partner defines the word and then finds the word in the passage. The partner substitutes his or her definition for the word and reads the sentence aloud. Both partners decide whether the sentence and the definition make sense.

Six-Way Paragraphs and Six-Way Paragraphs in the Content Areas

- high-interest nonfiction
- reading levels 1 to 12
- expository reading skills
- skills for reading textbooks
- self-assessment, self-scoring

English, Yes!

The selections in English, Yes! include a mixture of traditional and contemporary adapted classic literature. The instructional design accommodates both independent and cooperative learning. Students build proficiency with comprehension skills, vocabulary (including idioms), and grammar while improving their listening, speaking, and writing skills. Self-scoring exercises motivate students to continue to improve in language learning. A teacher's guide and a set of audiocassette tapes accompany each of the seven levels of the program.

English, Yes!

- literature-based program
- seven ESL levels
- comprehension skills
- vocabulary and idioms
- listening, speaking, and writing

Reading Fluency

The purpose of Reading Fluency is to help students become accurate, fluent readers. Fluent readers read at a good rate, with accuracy and proper intonation and phrasing. Fluency requires the reader to have good decoding skills; knowledge of the strategies to use in reading real text; and comprehension, which enables the reader to monitor what is being read to make sure it sounds like language. Reading Fluency includes seven *Readers* and seven *Reader's Record* books. Student placement is based on the student's independent reading level, which is the reading level at which the student feels comfortable. The instructional model in this series is that of repeated reading: A student reads a passage from the *Reader* to a partner. The partner checks off errors in the *Reader's Record.* Students then compute the reader's correct-words-per-minute score. The student reads the same passage a second time to produce a more fluent reading. Students evaluate their readings and record their correct-words-per-minute scores on the progress graphs in their own individual books.

Reading Fluency

- fiction and nonfiction reading passages
- reading levels 3 to 9
- self-evaluation and scoring
- focused fluency practice

Comprehension Skills

The Comprehension Skills series—*Understanding the Main Idea, Making Judgments, Understanding Literary Forms, Understanding Significant Details, Recognizing Tone, Understanding Characters, Understanding Organization, Making Inferences, Drawing Conclusions,* and *Understanding Vocabulary*—helps students to develop ten important reading-comprehension skills. Each book is divided into five parts that provide complete instruction and practice opportunities for the student:

Explanation—The skill is introduced, defined, and thoroughly explained.

Instruction—A detailed lesson on the skill is provided.

Sample Exercise—Students have a first try at using the skill and completing the exercises; students are guided step by step through an analysis of the answers.

Practice Exercises—Twenty practice exercises are available for student practice, gauged according to level of difficulty.

Writing Activities—Several writing activities are available for students to explore and apply the skill they have learned.

Comprehension Skills

- focused skills instruction
- reading levels 3 to 12
- 20 passages and exercises per book
- writing exercises
- CD component

Reading with Jamestown

The Contemporary Reader

Volumes 1 and 2 of The Contemporary Reader each includes six books with reading levels from 2.5 to 5. The six books in Volume 3 are at reading levels 6 through 8. The general-interest topics and paperback format make the books especially appealing to older readers. There is an activity-based teacher resource book for each volume. In addition to teaching suggestions, the *Teacher Resource Book* includes two reproducible exercise pages for each lesson—one focusing on vocabulary and the other on reading comprehension. Volumes 1 and 2 are accompanied by a set of three audiocassettes containing four selections from each book. Volume 3 has its own set of compact discs.

WordShop

Each book in WordShop offers 36 instructional lessons that cover a total of 360 words. The three types of lessons are Context Clues lessons, Theme lessons, and Root lessons. Each lesson provides opportunities for students to apply their understanding of the words in a reading or writing situation. Students are also introduced to appropriate variant forms of the words. A dictionary in the back of each book includes every vocabulary word studied in that book. Following every third lesson is a two-page test that covers the words in the three previous lessons. The Annotated Teacher Edition includes four more tests, each covering nine lessons.

Fright Write

Fright Write is designed to help all students have positive experiences with writing assignments. Fright Write books present writing assignments that are intriguing and imaginative. Each of the four Fright Write books is organized around a theme, and the ten lessons for each book lead students through the writing process to create products in a variety of genres. These include a suspense story, an audio recording, a screenplay, and a comic strip. A single *Teacher Guide* provides lesson plans for all four books plus two reproducible activity masters for each lesson—one in reading and one in writing.

The Contemporary Reader

- high-interest topical nonfiction
- three volumes, 18 books
- reading levels 2.5 to 8
- vocabulary and reading comprehension

WordShop

- vocabulary enrichment
- reading levels 6 to 8
- test-taking strategies
- periodic assessment and assessment record

Fright Write

- integrated reading and writing
- high-interest, suspenseful fiction
- reading levels 6 to 8
- focus on writing process and styles

Reading with Jamestown

Jamestown Placement Test

The Jamestown Placement Test (pages 79–81) will help you determine at which level—introductory, middle, or advanced—your students should be placed to receive maximum benefit from Jamestown materials.

Administering the Test

This silent reading comprehension test will take approximately 20 minutes. It is not timed, so allow time for most students to finish. Collect your students' test-answer sheets as they finish. Tell students that they may skip any question that is too difficult for them to answer. The Jamestown Placement Test may be duplicated for student use.

Answer Key for Student Placement Test			
1. b	5. b	9. b	13. c
2. b	6. b	10. c	14. c
3. a	7. c	11. a	15. a
4. b	8. a	12. d	

Student Placement Level Based on Score

Student Score	Placement Level
Number correct 8–10	Introductory
Number correct 10–13	Middle
Number correct 13–15	Advanced

Use your knowledge of each student's abilities to place students who receive a transitional score—10 or 13—in a level that is challenging without being discouraging.

For students scoring 7 or fewer correct, use the introductory level only in tutoring situations or when individualized help is available.

For students scoring at the advanced level on this placement test, examples of appropriate Jamestown materials are Jamestown's Reading Improvement Series: *Reading Drills—Advanced Level; Signature Reading—Levels I–L,* and *Six-Way Paragraphs—Advanced Level.*

Difficulty Levels of Jamestown Materials

This table lists the appropriate placement of students in Jamestown materials, based on Placement Test results. Book readability grade levels are also listed.

Title	Book Readability Grade Level	Jamestown Test Placement Level
Reading Drills, Fry		
Introductory	4–6	Introductory
Middle	6–8	Middle
Advanced	7–10	Advanced
Skimming and Scanning, Fry		
Middle	4–6	Middle
Advanced	7–9	Advanced
Vocabulary Drills, Fry		
Introductory	4–6	Introductory
Middle	6–8	Middle
Advanced	7–10	Advanced
Signature Reading		
Level D	2–4	Introductory
Level E	3–5	Introductory
Level F	4–6	Introductory
Level G	5–7	Middle
Level H	6–8	Middle
Level I	7–9	Advanced
Level J	8–10	Advanced
Level K	9–11	Advanced
Level L	10–12	Advanced
Six-Way Paragraphs		
Introductory	1–4	Introductory
Middle	4–8	Middle
Advanced	8–12	Advanced
Six-Way Paragraphs in the Content Areas		
Introductory	4–7	Introductory
Middle	7–10	Middle
Advanced	10–12+	Advanced

Title	Book Readability Grade Level	Jamestown Test Placement Level
WordShop		
Level F	6	Introductory
Level G	7	Middle
Level H	8	Advanced
Fright Write		
All	6–8	Middle/Advanced
Five-Star Stories, Goodman		
Travels/More Travels	1	Introductory
Adventures/More Adventures	2	Introductory
Chills/More Chills	3	Introductory
Surprises/More Surprises	4	Introductory
Shocks/After Shocks	5	Introductory/Middle
Sudden Twists/More Twists	6	Middle
Encounters/More Encounters	7	Middle
Conflicts/More Conflicts	8	Middle/Advanced
Choices	9	Advanced
Discoveries	10	Advanced
The Wild Side		
All	4–6	Introductory
Critical Reading Series		
All	6–8	Middle/Advanced
The Contemporary Reader		
Volumes 1 and 2: No. 1	2–3	Introductory
No. 2	2–3	Introductory
No. 3	3–4	Introductory
No. 4	3–4	Introductory
No. 5	4–5	Middle
No. 6	4–5	Middle
Volume 3: All	6–8	Middle/Advanced
Jamestown's American Portraits		
All	5–8	Middle/Advanced

Title	Book Readability Grade Level	Jamestown Test Placement Level
Best Nonfiction		
Introductory	5–6	Introductory
Middle	7–8	Middle
Advanced	9–12	Advanced
Best Poems		
Introductory	5–6	Introductory
Middle	7–8	Middle
Advanced	9–12	Advanced
Best Plays		
Introductory	5–6	Introductory
Middle	7–8	Middle
Advanced	9–12	Advanced
Best Short Stories		
Introductory	5–6	Introductory
Middle	6–8	Middle
Advanced	9+	Advanced
Best-Selling Chapters		
Introductory	5–6	Introductory
Middle	6–8	Middle
Advanced	9+	Advanced
Themes in Reading		
All	6–8	Middle/Advanced
Topics from the Restless		
Book One	6–7	Middle
Book Two	8–9	Middle
Book Three	10–11	Advanced
Book Four	12+	Advanced
Selections from the Black		
Book One	6–7	Middle
Book Two	8–9	Middle
Book Three	10–11	Advanced
Book Four	12+	Advanced

Jamestown Placement Test

Name _____	Date _____
Class _____	Score (Number Correct) _____

Directions

Read the passage. Then read each question and fill in the circle before the correct answer. You may look back at the passage. You may skip a question if the question is too difficult. Raise your hand when you are finished, and your teacher will collect the test.

On a calm, clear December afternoon in 1945, Flight 19 took off from the south coast of Florida on a routine Navy training mission. The five Avenger planes that made up Flight 19 would never return. Incredibly, a Martin Mariner plane sent to rescue Flight 19 was also lost without a trace.

Whenever planes or ships disappear in the infamous Bermuda Triangle, the wildest stories are heard. Many people think that the waters off the coast of Florida are the deadliest in the world. Legends tell of hundreds of ships and airplanes simply disappearing in the Bermuda Triangle.

1. Navy Flight 19 took off from
   ○ a. Bermuda.
   ○ b. Florida.
   ○ c. a Navy aircraft carrier.

2. How many planes made up Flight 19?
   ○ a. three
   ○ b. five
   ○ c. seven

3. Flight 19 was on a
   ○ a. training mission.
   ○ b. secret mission.
   ○ c. rescue mission.

4. The Bermuda Triangle is interesting because
   ○ a. it has been proven very dangerous.
   ○ b. many people think it is dangerous.
   ○ c. the Navy expected trouble there.

5. One thing we know about Flight 19 is that
   ○ a. it was rescued by Martin Mariner.
   ○ b. it was lost forever.
   ○ c. it would not become part of the legend.

Go on

Jamestown Placement Test

Name _____

Day had broken exceedingly cold and gray when the man turned aside from the main Yukon trail and climbed the high earthbank, where a dim and little-traveled trail led eastward through the fat spruce timberland. It was a steep bank, and he paused for breath at the top, excusing the act to himself by looking at his watch. It was nine o'clock. There was no sun nor hint of sun, though there was not a cloud in the sky. It was a clear day, and yet there seemed an intangible pall over the face of things, a subtle gloom that made the day dark, and that was due to the absence of sun. This fact did not worry the man. He was used to the lack of sun in this first season of the year. It had been days since he had seen the sun, and he knew that a few more days must pass before that cheerful orb, due south, would just peep above the skyline and dip immediately from view.

6. This story takes place
   - ○ a. in Siberia.
   - ○ b. in the Yukon Territory.
   - ○ c. during an Arctic expedition.

7. In what season is the story set?
   - ○ a. winter
   - ○ b. fall
   - ○ c. spring

8. The sky above the man was
   - ○ a. clear and cloudless.
   - ○ b. bright with sunlight.
   - ○ c. dim and cloudy.

9. What did the man see around him?
   - ○ a. wild animals
   - ○ b. trees
   - ○ c. barren land

10. The man may be described as
   - ○ a. scared.
   - ○ b. depressed.
   - ○ c. unafraid.

Go on

Jamestown Placement Test

Name _____

The Yellow Emperor was an important god in ancient times. He was a very powerful figure and had many children, some of whom were gods and some humans. He took great interest in the human race. Because he protected them and helped them to lead a peaceful, settled life, he was often considered to be an earthly emperor, the first to rule over China.

One of his greatest deeds was his defeat of a monster named Chiyou.

Chiyou started life as quite a lowly god. His task was to be a runner for the Yellow Emperor, one who cleared the way for him when he went on a journey. Chiyou was, however, very ambitious, and he planned to overthrow the Yellow Emperor and take his throne. Chiyou gathered as his followers some 80 minor gods who were discontented with the Yellow Emperor's reign.

---

11. Who was Chiyou?
    - ○ a. a lowly god who served as a runner for the Yellow Emperor
    - ○ b. one of the Yellow Emperor's ministers
    - ○ c. the Yellow Emperor's rainmaker
    - ○ d. the thunder god

12. What did Chiyou want?
    - ○ a. to be a more important god
    - ○ b. to lead the Yellow Emperor's army
    - ○ c. to be the Yellow Emperor's assistant
    - ○ d. to overthrow the Yellow Emperor and take his throne

13. Chiyou gathered together some 80 minor gods who
    - ○ a. refused to join Chiyou.
    - ○ b. wanted their own kingdoms.
    - ○ c. were discontented with the Yellow Emperor's reign.
    - ○ d. were content to be minor gods.

14. What do you think of the Yellow Emperor?
    - ○ a. He did not care about his people.
    - ○ b. He wasn't a good warrior.
    - ○ c. He was a good ruler.

15. Chiyou may be described as
    - ○ a. ambitious.
    - ○ b. lazy.
    - ○ c. loyal.

STOP

IRA/NCTE

Standards for the English Language Arts

Teaching Tip

Use your Jamestown reading products to help your class meet the IRA/NCTE standards.

The vision guiding these standards is that all students must have the opportunities and resources to develop the language skills they need to pursue life's goals and to participate fully as informed, productive members of society. These standards assume that literacy growth begins before children enter school as they experience and experiment with literacy activities—reading and writing, and associating spoken words with their graphic representations. Recognizing this fact, these standards encourage the development of curriculum and instruction that make productive use of the emerging literacy abilities that children bring to school. Furthermore, the standards provide ample room for the innovation and creativity essential to teaching and learning. They are not prescriptions for particular curriculum or instruction. Although we present these standards as a list, we want to emphasize that they are not distinct and separable; they are, in fact, interrelated and should be considered as a whole.

1. Students read a wide range of print and nonprint texts to build an understanding of texts, of themselves, and of the cultures of the United States and the world; to acquire new information; to respond to the needs and demands of society and the workplace; and for personal fulfillment. Among these texts are fiction and nonfiction, classic and contemporary works.

2. Students read a wide range of literature from many periods in many genres to build an understanding of the many dimensions (e.g., philosophical, ethical, aesthetic) of human experience.

3. Students apply a wide range of strategies to comprehend, interpret, evaluate, and appreciate texts. They draw on their prior knowledge, their interactions with other readers and writers, their knowledge of word meaning and of other texts, their word identification strategies, and their understanding of textual features (e.g., sound-letter correspondence, sentence structure, context, graphics).

4. Student adjust their use of spoken, written, and visual language (e.g., conventions, style, vocabulary) to communicate effectively with a variety of audiences and for different purposes.

5. Students employ a wide range of strategies as they write and use different writing process elements appropriately to communicate with different audiences for a variety of purposes.

6 Students apply knowledge of language structure, language conventions (e.g., spelling and punctuation), media techniques, figurative language, and genre to create, critique, and discuss print and nonprint texts.

7 Students conduct research on issues and interests by generating ideas and questions, and by posing problems. They gather, evaluate, and synthesize data from a variety of sources (e.g., print and nonprint texts, artifacts, people) to communicate their discoveries in ways that suit their purpose and audience.

8 Students use a variety of technological and information resources (e.g., libraries, databases, computer networks, video) to gather and synthesize information and to create and communicate knowledge.

9 Students develop an understanding of and respect for diversity in language use, patterns, and dialects across cultures, ethnic groups, geographic regions, and social roles.

10 Students whose first language is not English make use of their first language to develop competency in the English language arts and to develop understanding of content across the curriculum.

11 Students participate as knowledgeable, reflective, creative, and critical members of a variety of literacy communities.

12 Students use spoken, written, and visual language to accomplish their own purposes (e.g., for learning, enjoyment, persuasion, and the exchange of information).

Standards for the English Language Arts, by the International Reading Association and the National Council of Teachers of English. Copyright 1996 by the International Reading Association and the National Council of Teachers of English. Reprinted with permission.

Glossary

Activating Prior Knowledge—the reader's process of thinking about what he or she already knows about a topic, as a means of preparing for reading. Teachers activate prior knowledge by posing questions to draw out what students know about key ideas in what they will read.

Choral Reading—the reading in unison of parts of a selection by designated groups of students; especially effective with poetry and with prose that utilizes repetition.

Clarifying—a reading strategy that calls for the reader to make sure that text is understood—by rereading information, reading ahead, or consulting another source.

Concept Map—a graphic organizer in which ideas are organized, often in categories, around a central concept; also called a web.

Connecting—a reading strategy that calls for making connections between what was read and the reader's life, other books, and the world.

Context Clues—the clues to the meaning of an unfamiliar word that are provided in the words and sentences that surround that word. There are several types of context clues.

Decoding—using the knowledge of the sounds associated with letters and letter combinations to "sound out" a word; to say a word, using knowledge of letter-sound correspondence.

Echo Reading—text is read aloud, first by an accomplished reader and then by others who follow along while looking at the printed text.

Explicit Instruction—targeted and specific instruction. Explicit instruction often follows the cycle of introducing a strategy, modeling its use, guiding students as they practice the strategy, and then releasing students to use the strategy independently.

Fluency—smooth, accurate reading of text at a steady pace and with appropriate expression.

Graphic Organizers—a means of graphically representing ideas; structured formats for recording information about a selection, usually during or after reading.

Guided Reading—reading (individually, in small groups, or as a whole class) with active assistance from the teacher. During guided reading, the teacher questions students to be sure key ideas are understood and also models and guides the use of reading strategies.

KWL (What I *K*now, What I *W*ant to Know, What I *L*earned)—an instructional activity with an accompanying graphic organizer, especially appropriate when reading expository texts. Students are required to activate their prior knowledge, to form questions about what they would like to learn from reading, and to record during and after reading the information that they learned.

Making Inferences—the reading skill of making logical assumptions during reading that are based on clues provided in a story or an expository text. Good readers continually make logical inferences as they read.

Modeling—the demonstration of a reading skill or strategy. Modeling often includes defining the skill or strategy, thinking aloud while applying it to a reading selection, and then turning the process over to students.

Monitoring Comprehension—being aware of one's own reading process and noticing when comprehension breaks down. Readers check their reading process by questioning themselves as they read. When necessary, readers "repair" the breakdown in their understanding by rereading, reading on, or seeking help from another person or a reference source.

Predicting—a reading strategy in which the reader uses clues in the text and prior knowledge to make logical assumptions about what will happen.

Previewing—a process for preparing to read, especially effective with expository selections. Previewing includes looking over a selection, noting the title and author, headings, graphic elements, and boldface terms.

Questioning—a reading strategy in which the reader asks silent questions, while reading, to ensure that he or she is understanding the text.

Reciprocal Teaching—in a group setting, the process of applying a series of specific strategies—summarizing, questioning, clarifying, and predicting—to increase comprehension of text during reading.

Responding—a reading strategy in which the reader reacts to what has been read.

Scaffold—a step that helps provide the basis for the next step. Scaffolding often refers to careful step-by-step instruction in which each stage of learning is dependent on the students' understanding of the step that came before.

Setting a Purpose for Reading—a reader's process of establishing a reading goal.

Summarizing—synthesizing the key ideas in a text and restating those ideas in one's own words and in a logical order.

Text Structure—the ways ideas are organized and presented, especially in expository text. Four common text structures are time order, classification, cause and effect, and comparison and contrast. Recognizing the text structure helps students anticipate the kinds of information they will encounter and helps them navigate through dense informational writing.

Visualizing—a reading strategy in which the reader uses the words of a text and his or her own imagination to picture what is being described.

Main-Ideas Map

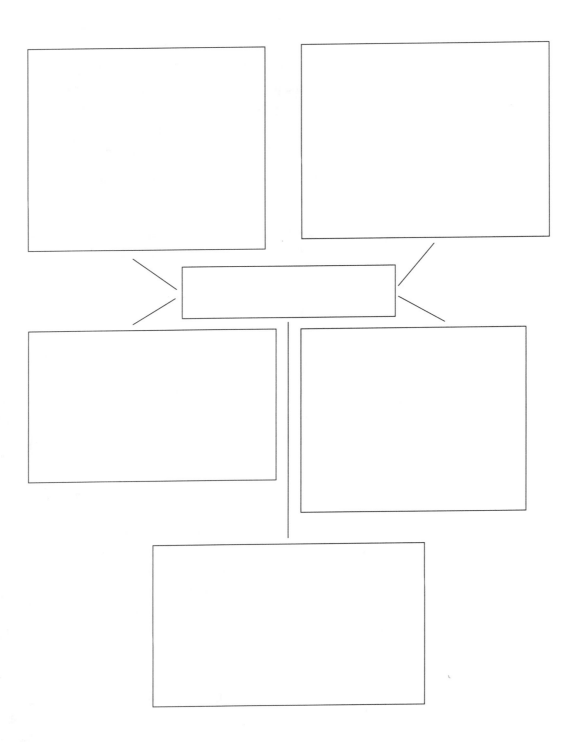

Flow Chart

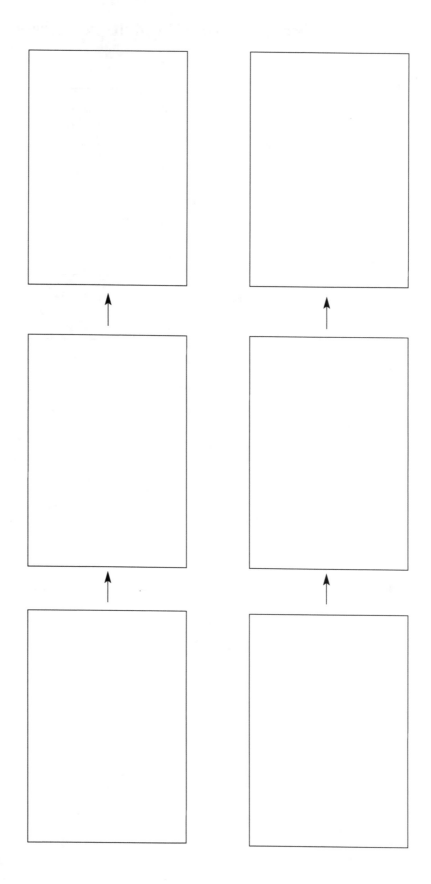

Single Cause with Multiple Effects

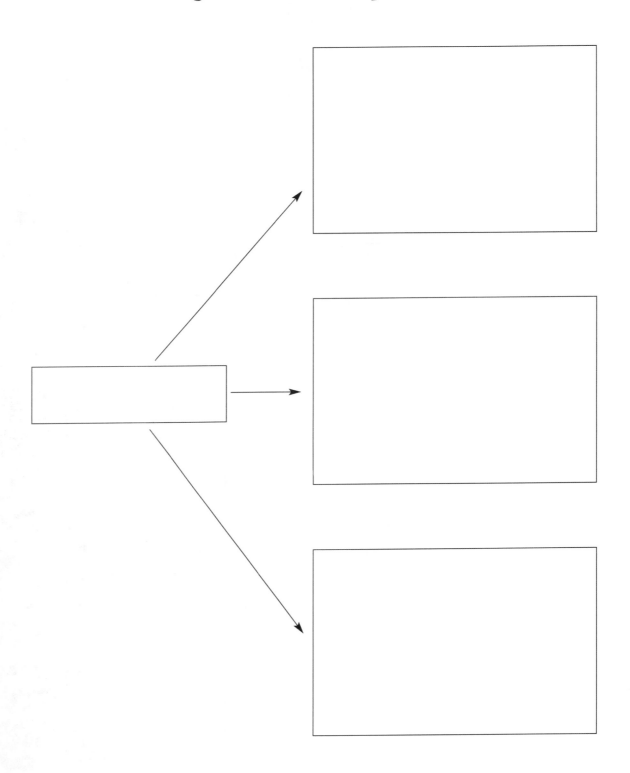

Cause-and-Effect Chain

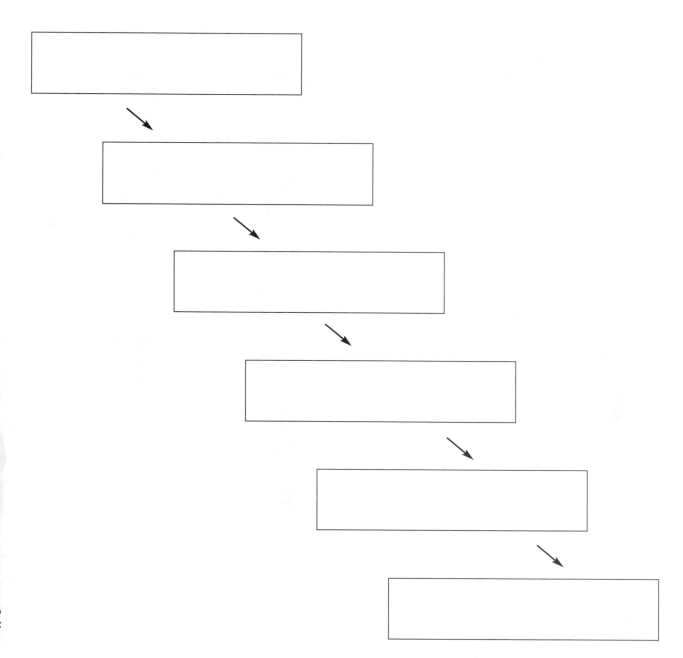

Venn Diagram

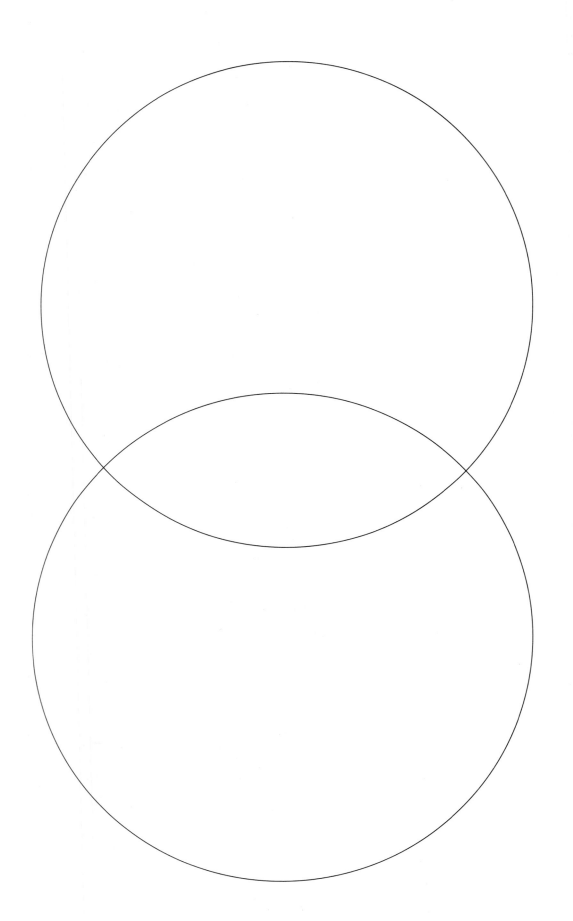